MY STORY, YOUR VOICE

DAVID SAMUELS

authorHOUSE®

AuthorHouse™
1663 Liberty Drive
Bloomington, IN 47403
www.authorhouse.com
Phone: 1 (800) 839-8640

Published by AuthorHouse 07/10/2018

ISBN: 978-1-5462-3203-2 (sc)
ISBN: 978-1-5462-3201-8 (hc)
ISBN: 978-1-5462-3202-5 (e)

Library of Congress Control Number: 2018903042

Print information available on the last page.

This book is printed on acid-free paper.

for permission contact David Samuels:

PO Box 391 Castries, Saint Lucia:
mrchairman2008@gmail.com
(758) 453-0062 (Home)
(758) 285-0430 (Mobile)

Cover design by Guillaume Rico
Photography- Bill Mortley (Front cover)Daniel Marcion-(Back cover)

TABLE OF CONTENTS

For Clerona, (Miss Na) my Grandmother, who gave so much and did everything to please me...What a priceless gem!And for the handful who have never stopped believing in me....

PREFACE

I started thinking about writing during 2012 and contacted Guy Ellis, at the time the editor of the Mirror newspaper. We subsequently met and discussed what form the book should take. I didn't give any consideration then to an autobiography, but had some ideas about transcribing and publishing some interviews I'd recorded over the years with some high profile persons, including Sir John Compton, Dr. Kenny Anthony and George Odlum.

Some time later, while on a visit to my home, photographer Bill Mortley during a discussion commented "You know you have a few books in you?" Somewhat taken by surprise, I asked him to elaborate and after he did, kept thinking about that possibility and randomly began making notes about the early years living with my Grandmother, as my Mother had left me in her care to pursue my father in England to end the sham marriage to him. I was just about 6 or 7 years old and attended the RC Boys Infant and from there Primary and then later the Senior School just a stone's throw away.

I spent a few years as a vocalist with the Tru Tones, arguably the leading dance band in Saint Lucia at the time and during that same period went into the broadcasting profession with the Windward Islands Broadcasting Service (WIBS) which in 1972, mushroomed into Radio Saint Lucia, (RSL) but just before that, an enjoyable 3 year stint with Radio Caribbean International. (RCI)

Apart from my initial years in radio, the most rewarding time spent was with Caribbean Hotel Management Services, (CIIMS) operated by Bill Stewart and Theo Gobat, confronting the challenges of running four hotels as their Public Relations and Entertainment Director; Halcyon Days in Vieux Fort, (now Coconut Bay) Halcyon Sands on Vigie Beach, Halcyon Beach Club at Choc (now Sandals Halcyon) and the Saint Lucian Hotel on Reduit Beach. After four years there, I moved over to Cunard La Toc Hotel and Suites in a similar position in 1982 and spent over six years there and that is where appreciation of the importance of the tourist industry really grew. The chapter "Cunard Bytes" explains it all.

During my time at Cunard, I was being sought regularly by a number of businesses and some advertising agencies to "script and voice" radio and television commercials, but I didn't have a production studio and that's how David Samuels Promotions and Video Productions (DSP) came into being, with the support of Andrew Hulsmeier who owned a similar operation in Barbados and the main person behind many of my earlier productions like "Images of St. Lucia" and "Fun in Paradise St. Lucia", as well as innumerable Infomercials, Documentaries and Television Commercials, which made us one of the leading production facilities in the Eastern Caribbean region. Special mention should also be made of my camera crew led by Fimbar Anius (passed in 2016) and John Anius, with assistance from his brother Thomas from time to time. I'm tremendously grateful to all of them for the incredible, amazing and absolutely successful role they played in the company-1988-1999. DSP earned several national awards during that time, for Television commercials and other productions, Music Record Productions and a pocket sized Tourism publication and Skyview maps. Those were the "Glory Years" indeed!

In 1996, during construction of my home/business complex at Morne Fortune, there appeared to be some strong occultic activity which caused me great anxiety and distress, resulting in many aspects of the construction being left incompleted, coupled with some bizarre occurrences of an indescribable dark dimension but for the spiritual guidance of some Roman Catholic priests and the grace of God, my life would have been cut short as explained in the chapter "The Job Man".

By the year 2000, I was conflicted about remaining in the business because by then I had lost my "Mojo" and was somewhat drained emotionally, creatively and financially. My trust and faith in those around me depleted. I considered a return to broadcasting if only for a short time and that is how I ended up at Radio Saint Lucia in 2002. By then a lot had changed in the broadcasting landscape, as excellence, professionalism and production standards had diminished. However, I did my best in utilizing all the skills acquired in my earlier years at RSL. The politics too had changed and with it the "jobs for the boys" syndrome and I got the distinct impression that anyone who was part of the Compton era was marginalized and discarded. It was all very sad but it's the honest truth. See the chapter "Click" RSL 97!

As mentioned earlier, my Mom followed my Dad who had preceded her for England some 4 years earlier in 1953. Family had always been tight lipped about him whilst growing up from adolesence into adulthood. However, I was able to put bits of the puzzle together about this enigmatic man, who had left a few broken hearted women with children behind in his native Antigua, marries my Mom in Saint Lucia, then walked out on us and carried on in the same vein in England and finally Germany, where I learned in 2013, that I had three brothers and five sisters. It is because of one of my sisters, Bettina, also Vincent, a nephew in St. Thomas, in the United States Virgin Islands (U.S.V.I.), that I was able to relate the story of my father, David Z and family, in the chapter "Passages". There's some unbelievable stuff in there that movies are made out of...

When I thought of the inclusion of a chapter on Saint Lucian Calypso, I was advised that it would not compliment the autobiographical theme in the strictest sense. "The book will lose its relevance" an editor remarked, but I argued, "Why should it?" The reader will recognize and come to understand why I wanted to do this; it remains my firm belief that Calypso, basically provided some insight into my understanding of the Saint Lucian Psyché. The interviews with Multi Monarch Winner Desmond *Pep* Long and prolific writer Nahum *Happy* Jn Baptiste and the inclusion of some lyrics by them, including Jeff *Pelay* Elva, Ignatius *Invader* Tisin, Herman *Ashanti* Hippolyte, *Menell* Delice, Sylvester *Herb Black* Lewis and Mark *Lord Jackson* Philips in "Dear Calypso," will silence the naysayers and enhance your love for calypso.

The chapter on Mr. Chairman describes some of what I've had to endure during the presentation of the show at Calabash Television (CTV), including some perspective on Saint Lucian politics, ending with a highlight on the three most popular guests since the program's inception in 2013. The Odlum Chapter is a master stroke of tenacity and digging and thinking deep into my being as a result of the unfortunate loss of the original interview on compact disc, but it all worked out a lot better than I'd expected.

Finally, the interviews with Dame Pearlette Louisy who reflects on her 20 year tenure as Saint Lucia's Governor General; the absorbing discourse with former Prime Minister Sir John, in 2004, just before returning to politics; Prime Minister Dr. Anthony Live! just 5 days before the 2006 General Elections and finally Prime Minister Allen Chastanet, who brings the country several doses of hope and optimism - that the best days are ahead of us.

It was quite an experience speaking to all of them on your behalf and students of political history and some in academia will find the accounts of their experiences absolutely fascinating and in some cases riveting. Overall, writing the book involved a lot of personal sacrifices, research, late nights and extremely long hours but its been a labour of love and commitment and without hesitation, I'd do it all over again.

Finally, I've never considered my voice as my own, but belonging to Saint Lucia and its people whom I have always tried to seek answers to myriad questions when interviewing a broad range of people on radio and television. So it's my hope that this modest effort meets with your approval.

Happy reading!

ACKNOWLEDGEMENTS

Acknowledgement and thanks must go to several individuals who helped me along the way in the completion of this wonderful but challenging task.

The late Frank Norville for discovering and encouraging me to pursue my ambition as a singer in the late 60's and early 70's

Ronald Boo Hinkson:
Chester Hinkson:-For nuturing my talent as a vocalist in the Tru Tones Band during my youthful years

Winston Hinkson, Margaret Roberts-Steele: For introducing me to broadcasting and providing me with the initial tools for success.

Harold George: A great source of inspiration and assistance during the WIBS/Early RSL era.

Leslie Clarke: For your guidance and support.
Emelda Charles: My go to person, during the early years at Radio Caribbean International (RCI).

William Bill Stewart, Theo Gobat: Responsible for my introduction to the Tourist Industry at Halcyon Beach Club-The meca of Saint Lucian entertainment throughout the 70's/80's.

To all those who made David Samuels Promotions and Video Productions the household name it became: Fimbar Anius (deceased) John Anius,

Thomas Anius, Gregory Dixon, Carol Warner, *Andrew Hulsmeire, Stuart Jenkins, Norman Barrow, Keith/Sally Miller (*all from Barbados)

The Radio Saint Lucia staff: Especially Oliver J Lawrence, Ms. Mary Polius, Delorne Edole, Medalise Breen and Steve,

Guy Ellis: For editorial guidance during the initial stages of the publication.

Jerry George: Thanks for your enthusiastic contributions, unwavering interest, guidance, support and for being a good friend.

Mrs. Loyola Devaux: For your editorial and proofreading professionalism, especially when I was faced with insurmountable challenges. Thanks also for your wonderful introduction.

Ms. Lilia Albert and the wonderful staff at Infinity Desktop Publishing and Typing Services Ltd. on Micoud Street. "I will always be eternally grateful!"

Fr. Lambert St. Rose: Thanks for your thought provoking contribution in the *Job Man Chapter*, as well as your spiritual guidance and prayers over the years. Mention too of Fr. Goodman, Fr. Quinlan and Fr. Toss.

Bill Mortley: Excellence personified! Providing the photographs on the front cover and other areas in the book.

Marcion-Belle Portwe: For providing photographs on the grounds of Government House during the National Awards Ceremony in February, 2017. As well as the use of the photo on the back cover and others in the book.

Guillame Rico: For creating the Front and Back cover design of the book. What extraordinary talent you have. My grateful thanks!

Ian Sanchez: Thanks for providing some personal tidbits on the late Pelay (Jeff Elva)

Nahum Jn Baptiste: Thanks for your enthusiasm, friendship and participation in the chapter "Dear Calypso". My thanks also to Pep (Desmond Long) and Papa Vader (Ignatius Tisin) for their eager participation in the project.

Sister Rayneau and the Marian Home staff, for providing a place of refuge for my grandmother and mother during their final months on this earth. My eternal gratitude and my promise to donate a portion of the book sales to the home annually.

Jeannie/Albert Beausoliel: For your critical assessment of some of the chapters and your wonderful and genuine friendship.

The Ministry of Culture and its indefatigable Minister, Senator Fortuna Belrose...as well as Permanent Secretary, Donovan Williams.

Castries Mayor, Peterson Francis and the Castries Constituency Council (CCC)
Sam Augier (SMJ Beverages)
Oswald Augustin
Michael Chastanet

And finally, to GOD be the GLORY, for being there for me every step along the way. "GOD is the source of my inspiration".

INTRODUCTION

MY STORY, YOUR VOICE

Life! What is it all about? Often we wonder.

Each of us has been born into a family setting of some kind. However, each family setting is unique and different in many ways. From the poorest families to the richest families, there are hurdles and difficulties to deal with as well as good times with gatherings of family and friends. Such togetherness enhances our disposition and sets us on a proper course for life. There are times though when we have to 'go it alone' in order to succeed.

David Samuels presents us with a portfolio of a variety of opportunities and people who have passed in and out throughout his lifetime. He is a well known radio personality and TV Talk Show Host as well as an entrepreneur over many years. He also worked in the tourism industry for over a decade and then established his own public relations, advertising and video production company (DSP) which he ran for some time. My Story, Your Voice gives us an opportunity to appreciate many aspects and people of our country, Saint Lucia, through the interesting information and presentations of David Samuels.

Mrs. Loyola Devaux
Assistant Editor
Former Lecturer of
Sir Arthur Lewis Community College (S.A.L.C.C.)

FOREWORD

Before the end of 2017, at a ceremony I attended, the speaker stated (paraphrase): the richest archives are our cemeteries. I thought about this for a few days and once past the morbid nurture of cemeteries, I had to admit to this truism; that each tombstone in a cemetery represents, for the most part, an untold story. I also thought of how much enriched our lives could have been from the insights we would have gleaned from the thousands of stories if they had been told. Take for example, hundreds of Saint Lucian women carried large trays of rock from the mountain that had been blasted to give way for the approach for landing at Sir George F.L. Charles airport at Vigie; and these rocks were used as the foundation of the runway as we now know it, which runs parallel to the main cemetery in Castries.

I am glad that my media colleague, David Samuels, has shared his life story with us before it ended up untold in the cemetery. He has now joined quite a few Saint Lucians who have recently decided to put pen to paper and tell their own stories or share their perspectives on Saint Lucian life.

Dave's story is both intriguing and inspiring. Intriguing in the sense that the real lives of Saint Lucians, like Dave, who become a household name through their voices on the radio, are seldom known. The public is lured into a fascination with the sound and smoothness of their voices and the rest of their lives are snippets of innuendo, untruths and rumour which usually snowballed into becoming "the truth". Dave is one of only a few in the media who has taken the bold step to fill in the gaps with facts. I am glad that I had a hand in pushing Dave in that direction. Sometime in early 2014, I wrote a tribute to Mr. Samuels (Respect due Mr. Chairman) on my Facebook page. One of the outcomes of the feedback from readers was a call to tell his life story in a book. One of those responding to my tribute was Justice Gregory Regis, who worked with Dave in the early days of Radio Saint Lucia and who now resides in Canada. He said: "Our people have never developed the practice (culture) of respecting and honouring their people. I'm so glad you have done this. Dave has consistently produced high quality work. It speaks volumes about his personality and commitment to his profession that he has maintained such professional integrity in the present atmosphere in Saint Lucia." Here it is.

From the young boy who felt abandoned to rising to be one of our nation's respected broadcasters and entrepreneurs. His parents had moved, in search of a better life and he was left in the care of his grandmother. This still happens. His late mother may not have agreed on abandonment, perhaps, and would say this was a tough choice that had to be made. The sacrifice was made in the hope that the search for greener pastures overseas would have redounded to a happier life for all. For many, this wasn't the case. In fact, Dave didn't see his mother for many years and his father left when he was still a tot. And so, Dave had to rise above this with the guidance of his grandmother, whom he speaks of with tenderness and sentimentality and at the same time as if she was the hero in his life. It is because of her positive outlook on life and for him that Dave seems to have overcome obstacles where the results could have been different. "Don't worry", she would tell him in facing any of life's obstacles, "they are not God…let God deal with them."

There is much to learn about the times that shaped him as a young man; the meeting of his family in Antigua and Tortola and finally meeting his German born sister Bettina – but still not having met with his biological father before he died. His final moments with his mother – as if hearing an inner voice calling him back to her bedside before her passing - are especially touching.

I have said in my tribute that were David Samuels in another country he would have been honoured countless times for his grit, his determination and contribution to our nation's well-being. It is true that he received the

Saint Lucia Medal of Merit (Order of Saint Lucia Awards) in 2017, and recognized for his "contribution to broadcasting". But his contributions traverse other fields: music and entertainment, tourism and hospitality, public relations/media, public affairs. Thankfully, in his book he chronicles his rise in each of these areas. It is the story of a self-made man, that, to me, is remarkable…who was an entrepreneur even before that word took on its current lofty accolade and currency. Is that about being lucky and being at the right place at the right time? The reader will decide. But what for me is most important is that the book can be a great help for others seeking a path to success. On their own terms as we see examples unfolded in this book.

Readers who follow Saint Lucian politics will find the conversations in interviews with well-known Saint Lucian leaders to be revealing. One area of his career in broadcasting, that spans over 40 years, is to be recognized as one of Saint Lucia's best media interviewers. The reader is provided with a transcript of these interviews, rather than spoon fed an interpretation or an opinion.

This book will certainly add to your knowing David Samuels better, no doubt. But it will also give much to think about. Well done, Dave!

JEREMY E.M. GEORGE

CHAPTER 1

ALPHA

"Man is of the earth."

The decade of the 1950s marked the beginning of a defining era in the history of Saint Lucia and I consider myself fortunate to have been born in the opening year of that era. The Second World War had ended five years before, the then town of Castries razed by a great fire three years later and the political and social awakening that had started in Saint Lucia in the 1930s was heading towards a kind of climax.

Up to that time, indeed from 1925, the right to vote and to be elected was enjoyed by only a small section of the population who had property and money. According to A HISTORY OF SAINT LUCIA (Harmsen, Ellis and Devaux, 2012) "on the eve of the introduction of universal adult suffrage, just 2,553 people were eligible to vote out of a population of some 79,500 souls." However, 1950, thankfully ushered in meaningful change. Britain gave Saint Lucia and the other Windward Islands a new constitution along with adult suffrage and everyone 21 years and over, regardless of social or economic circumstances, was given the right to vote.

This was the climate in which I came to be born on 26th. April, 1950, in a little house at the northern end of Chaussee Road smack opposite the entrance to the Botanical Gardens or George V Park. My father, David Zachary Samuels, was Antiguan and my mother, Marcienne Julietta

Isidore, from Saint Lucia. I have no knowledge of the details of the three years they spent together after marrying but from what I have been able to gather, even from my mother, it is fair to say that their relationship was far from perfect. When it comes to my early childhood, I have no recollection of my father and only two vivid memories of my mother when I was growing up. One was of her being ill and having to be hospitalized. I may have been about five years old and the second was when she left for England in 1957.

It was very cold as my grandmother and I walked to the northern wharf in the wee hours of the morning to bid my mother farewell. I can still remember the M.V. "Ascania" as she departed the docks, with mom waving goodbye to us at the side of the vessel. Thus my world came crashing down again, as my father had preceded her to England four years earlier. Why had they left me? What had I done? Didn't they love me? I was confused, frightened and I think in a sense, my life changed that day.

As a consequence of that early abandonment, my formative years were traumatic. I remember always being alone. After my mother went to England, I lived in the "CDC", an urban housing project that had sprung up in the aftermath of the fire in 1948. Around 1957, there were lots of neighbours around. I remember playing a lot on my own - cricket and some football in the neighbourhood. My grandmother was understandably very protective of me and did not want me to wander off too far because you know as children, when you were sent on an errand "to make message" in local parlance, the items were usually written on a piece of paper for the proprietor. We would usually take the opportunity to stop here and there along the way, and so I did, to and from Mr. Boy's Bakery along a very narrow track just behind the Hyacinth family home on High Street. Mr. Hyacinth was a well known tailor in the neighborhood. Next door was the "Herald Newspaper", where you could always listen to the latest cricket score over the radio, which was usually played quite loudly, or to purchase some salt fish, luncheon meat, condensed milk and other small items from "Maggi's Grocery Shop" at the corner of Coral and High Streets right across from Block Z. If Granny did not see me for a while, she would come out looking for me.

I always felt that I was under her wings so to speak, so much so that my friends used to tease me about it. I remember them making fun of me quite a lot, but my main recollection of that time was of always feeling alone. I did not have family around me like other neighbourhood children and I often wondered how it was that I had no parents, no siblings, even my grandmother I found very cagey whenever I enquired about that. Later, I gathered that my parents were having issues in England, but as a little boy I was never given the truth, but that's how things were back then. You were a child and you could not be concerned with or involved in the affairs of grown-ups. My grandmother frequently attempted to appease me with the promise that my mother would speak to me when I was older. I do not recall ever being satisfied with that explanation, although I believe I must have been looking forward to the fulfillment of that promise.

The St. Aloysius R.C. Boys Infant School was on the bottom floor of a two storey crumbly looking wooden building with the big boys located upstairs. The entrance to the schools opened to a fairly large yard on Brazil Street. I believe that, for a little while, I may have resided in a wooden house which my Dad and Mom occupied to the right of the school's entrance, just prior to his move to England, before my Mom finally moved in with my grandmother in the CDC. The school was a great hub of activity and extremely noisy especially during recess and just before the bell rang to herald the start of the new day, or when school classes were dismissed.

Perhaps the most popular hang out for the students generally, was Cazaubon's Shop noted for it's lime squash and cakes: turnovers, buns, pone, rock cakes, etc, right at the corner of Brazil and Broglie streets, directly opposite Mr. Reggie's who was a short, dark, bespectacled man who specialized in merchandising school items like exercise books, slates and pencils on which infants would write, lead pencils, pens, rulers, erasers and the like...I remember how some of the boys would try to distract Reggie's attention at one end of the shop, while others would take away some items undetected. I was never certain if he was ever aware of all the goings on, and often wondered what was the extent of his losses. Then there was the traditional "School boy, School girl rivalry between the Ave Maria Girls', a stone's throw from Cazaubon's, and the R.C. Boys- I can still hear the chants *"RC Bon Bon Wasi"* (Stale Cake) to which the boys responded *"Ave Maria Tèt Chode Fanm Fol Déyé Yo"* a constant reminder no doubt of the fire, which had almost razed the top part of the school buildings housing the girls around 1958/59.

Every little Catholic boy and girl remembers his or her First Communion day and all the attention that was received. Even Miss Yvette Trim, now Nathaniel, my Stage Two teacher at the R.C. Boys Infant, says that she remembers me in her class at the age of 6 or 7 years old. What an obedient and good little boy I was, but a quiet little boy? I remember her and teachers like Ms Beryl, Ms. Sonia George, Ms Alicia John, Miss Carmen, and Ms Joseph the headmistress. Anyway, I was probably seven going on eight and the three day retreat preceded the big day. During that time we had to go through an exercise unlike anything that we'd ever done before. We were indoctrinated religiously: Bible stories, praying the rosary, prayers and more prayers including the rebuke of the devil "and all his works and pomps and I give myself to Jesus through the heart of Mary".

Then there was confession where we had to tell the priest all the naughty things a little boy does: cursing, cheating, stealing, lying, fighting etc. All of that before receiving Holy Communion. We went back and forth-from the school to the church, back to the school and then back home. It was a busy period and very important to a youngster who mirrored like his peers, 'Innocence to the max'. What an exciting week - especially the thought of the iced cakes and all the goodies that my little stomach was awaiting, as well as all the family members that were going to be present to celebrate the occasion made it even more exciting.

We spent a couple of hours in the church after the procession: white jacket, white vests, white shirt, white short pants, white socks with matching shoes and the imposing white bow just off the upper left shoulder. Then all the photos with family in church, outside church, on the Columbus Square (now Derek Walcott Square) and at the apartment in front of the First Communion table, then back to the church for a while. By the time you returned home you were exhausted, given some hot soup, bread and a glass of grape Fanta that was bottled by JQ Charles at the time and if you were lucky just a sip or two of Ruby red wine. Before dozing off you couldn't help being aware of all the merriment taking place outside your room: The peals of laughter, animated chatter complimented by the music of the day. In the blink of an eye, it was all over and normalcy returned all too quickly, but it wasn't a dream. It actually happened in January, 1959.

I am somewhat surprised that I did not become wayward because I had both motive and opportunity to follow bad company, adopt anti social habits and all kinds of deviant behavior, but for some reason, I did not. I do not know whether it was because I was strong…or because there were people in the area who attempted to keep me in check. Looking back I can see what an important role they played in my life, a role that they themselves might not have even been aware of. However, it was a double-edged sword because there were times when some of these very 'good Samaritans' took advantage of me with pranks of humiliation which they considered as a way of having fun but which impacted negatively on my self-esteem. There were certain things that they did to me which really hurt. I bore the humiliation, not being able to speak about it. You have to really try to understand the things I went through, like even going to visit my grandfather a short distance away on Brazil Street, but not really feeling the embrace of family there. Those meetings in the main were courteous and respectful but awkward, rigid, and devoid of what passes for family warmth and affection. After all, I was his only grandson then, but he fathered two sons and two daughters who were older than I was.

I remember, while attending the St. Aloysius R.C. Boys Primary School, a teacher saying to me that I had the opportunity to go as far as I possibly could because I was bright and eager to learn but only if I had someone to push me. I always wondered about that, because for some reason there wasn't anyone that I could depend on to help me to excel. I confronted negativity very early in life. Of course I did not understand it at the time, but in a way it was actually preparing me for the future.

I saw many children who lived in my area taking the wrong route but I never followed them. I was able to remain on the straight and narrow path without getting into any serious trouble. Some people have referred to me as being self-made and I have had the opportunity to think about that from time to time, because when you consider that I never really had any role models or people to motivate me, I do understand the commendation and it is very clear to me now more than ever, the significant role that my grandmother played in my life.

When I lived with my grandmother, Clerona Isidore, there were monthly remittances from my mother in England to take care of me. Sometimes it came late and on such occasions granny would give me a note to take to my grandfather who worked as head of the Inland Revenue Department on Constitution Park, seeking some bridging finance until the money order from England came. Most times he was busy and at times I would spend up to two hours waiting before he could see me. On occasions, staff in the department would come and call me in. Little things like that I found embarrassing. I honestly felt that my granddad had the opportunity to fill in the gap vacated by my parents, as "Jue", my mother was his first and only child with my grandmother. It appeared that the relationship fizzled after the birth of my mom.

Maybe it was the power of granny's prayers. While I don't recall hearing her pray, there was a Rosary that had found a permanent place in the pocket of her Singer Sewing Machine. I've never doubted that she was a very prayerful woman. There were times when I would share some of my problems with her and she would usually respond *"Pa Worry Ich Moi, Yo pas Bondye"*! Miss Na was a seamstress who sewed for a number of prominent people at the time. I recall them coming home to pick up their dresses, blouses and skirts and listened to some of the animated discussion. She would suggest, whenever I appeared, that they should speak in *"Patois"* as I did not understand. She'd say" *Parlais en patois y paca kopan,*" or so they thought. She was always there for me and gave me everything I needed. Sometimes I can still hear the machine going into the night through to the early hours of the next day. When ill with a headache, stomach upset or after a purge of the dreaded senna, and in some pain, she would bring me a cup of hot ginger, sour soup or spice tea. I could still feel her hands stroking my head while seated on the toilet bowl. That touch was ever so comforting.

It appeared that 'Julian' my grandfather, had been her one true love, and after the break-up for whatever reason she had decided to close that chapter on men and seek 'Her God!' – She took me to Sunday Mass and again to Vespers in the evening, and at times we went to the cinema at Clarke's or Gaiety's just a short distance away from the church and from our CDC apartment. I eagerly looked forward to her treat of fried black pudding with onions, herbs and spices on Sundays, plus a specially made ti-ponch during the Sunday Meal.

Granny was never the same after they discovered that she'd left an intrauterine contraceptive device ('IUD' also known as a Coil, a metal device) in her uterus. I suspect some time after the birth of my mother, it had infected her pancreas which had by then spread to other parts of the stomach. We didn't expect her to survive that but she went on to live for another 12 years.

Most of those years were spent with a relative of granny's who lived at the top of Pavee Road. Mom had requested her help in providing care for my grandmother which necessitated the building or extension of one of the rooms in the home. Cousin Martina did a fantastic job in nursing my granny, even though she didn't have any formal training in the field. I'm sure it wasn't easy, but she did her best in the circumstances.

Mom would often arrange for barrels of all of granny's needs, toiletries, clothing, etc. to be shipped to cousin Martina from Curacao. Granny was extremely happy to see me whenever I visited and seemed to know all that was happening in the country because of the television and radio that were constantly left on during the course of the day and she often expressed concern that she was not able to cook, wash and iron for me, which spoke of her maternal instinct so incredibly. After some years, Martina's children, especially Mauricia and Mable, began to express concern that their mother's health was deteriorating due mainly to diabetic complications, and so it was decided that some other arrangement needed to be made. With this in mind I approached the sisters at the Marian Home to find out if it was possible for them to facilitate granny there. Initially, it didn't seem there was any room, but the good Lord has a way of opening doors when they seem firmly shut. Hence that's how Miss Na ended up at the Marian Home in 1985, some eight years after residing at Pavee.

The October Holiday Weekend (1988) just before her death, I had gone to Barbados to work on a video project with Andrew Hulsmeier and had not known of her hospitalization prior to leaving. Having completed the project and despite insistence of friends in Barbados to stay for the Monday Holiday, I had this burning desire to return home.

On my return, I noticed that the light was blinking on my answering machine and the message by a sister at the home told of my grandmother's hospitalization, so I rushed to the hospital. She was asleep, so I went downtown to purchase some toiletries and other essentials. After that, I returned to Victoria Hospital and then drove to Micoud to visit Laurencia, a close friend, to express my woes about my grandmother's condition.

On my return from Micoud, I spent an hour or so with Granny. She was in a conscious / semi conscious state, and smiled broadly every time she woke up and saw me. She kept thanking me and my mother for all that we had done for her. I sensed that the end was near. Her hair was as white as wool and she looked so much at peace. I wanted to spend the night with her but the nurse on duty told me that I should go home to get some sleep and promised to call me immediately if there was any change. I left the hospital, somewhat reluctantly and must confess to having a restless and sleepless night. Very early next day at about 6:00 a.m., I received the inevitable call from the hospital informing me of her passing, just minutes before.

I contacted Mom in Curacao. She had just recovered from a bout of illness but recovered sufficiently to attend the funeral of her mother. She had lost some of her spunk and glow and seemed a little slower. Clearly the losses, the illnesses and hard knocks had taken their toll and it moved me to tears sometimes, although I was very careful not to show her that emotion. I was so thankful to be there for her which she often acknowledged. I have to say that granny's loss was heartfelt as she was the only real connection to family that I had. In many ways, granny was the only mother I knew.

So for the first time I had to adapt to doing household chores. That transition wasn't easy! I would soon miss her Godly wisdom and counsel, her lilting kweyol speaking, and the laughter which emanated from the hordes of customers and friends who dropped in regularly. Yes! I had to adapt and do so very quickly.

CHAPTER 2

BITTER SWEET

"It's not what goes in but rather what comes out, for as a man speaketh so is he". Regular saying of my Grandmother.

At the St. Aloysius R.C. Boys Primary School, the teachers were always asking me to come to the front of the class to relate stories to my peers, so maybe that is where the interest in broadcasting came from. I was also something of a dramatist. I remember performing in plays both at Infant and Primary School levels but by and large it appeared to be an uneventful period in my youthful years. I was able to work my way up to Scholarship Class and sat the Common Entrance Exams and passed to enter St. Mary's College at the age of 12 years.

I vividly remember my Headteacher Mr. Augustin *"Redhead"* St. Clair calling out the successful Entrance test students at Assembly and presenting us as the group from R.C. Boys that were going to St. Mary's. However, my father and mother were divorcing in England around that time, and my mother fell ill for months due to the stress created by the issues with my father, which impacted the receipt of the monthly remittances. In those days just about $16 a term was needed to send one to St. Mary's, a small sum that was considered a lot of money at the time and I was being told that I had to report to the school by a certain date with the funds. But lo and behold, I soon discovered I could not get into College because there was no money to finance the move. My grandfather had promised to chip in and my godparents Mr. and Mrs. Fitz St. Rose who lived at Hospital Road, said they would contribute, but on the condition that my grandfather helped, but sadly he reneged.

So I missed out on the opportunity at what was then and still is a top class institution. Fortunately, we had what was called the 'Senior School' which I attended for about three years. The school started on the top floor of the old Castries Parish Centre Building by the Catholic Authorities under Bishop Gachet in 1964, to provide academic and vocational opportunities to students who were unable to make it to secondary school due to financial constraints or were slow or late in their development for one reason or another. The curriculum included: English Language, English Literature, Mathematics, French, West Indian History, Geography, Industrial Arts, Home Economics, Crochet and Physical Education. The church also provided typewriters and so typing and short hand were taught by volunteers, notably Mrs. Mauricia Edward (nee Cazaubon) former employee of Scotia Bank and Mrs. Agatha Modeste. In many ways Senior School could have been described as "transformational" for a 1960's educational institution, as it was encouraged to design curricula that students might have some interest in. The staff adopted a new approach of challenging students to express their disagreements, though in a polite and respectful manner, as long as they could support their various positions. Some students were given special consideration and transferred to Form 3 of St. Mary's College and St. Joseph's Convent after a couple of years at the school.

Those were the years of "The Dedicated Teacher" and the following, some of whom are now deceased come to mind: Raymond John, Albert Nathaniel, Gregory Blanchard, Guy Duplessis, Rumelia Elwin, Roland Branch, Rosella Bushell, O.P. Jules and Mr. Gill of St. Mary's College. Then there was Bertilia Jn Baptiste, Martha Isaac, Agatha Modeste, Rosina Glasgow, Jacinta Anius Lee. The French language was taught by Roman Catholic Priests, Frs. Michel and Laurent. I recall fondly Physical Education with Rumelia who also taught us to appreciate the various dances and songs that were an integral part of our African, French and

British Ancestry. No wonder I got to love the indigenous music and dance of Saint Lucia so very much.

A number of Senior School Graduates entered the teaching, nursing, police, and banking professions, while others were recruited into the Air Travel Industry, media, hotel management, Trade Unionism and the Caribbean Development Bank. About 600 students passed through this institution which was closed in 1972, after a period of eight years, because government, through the Ministry of Education, started to emphasize Junior Secondary and Comprehensive Schools on the island. Whenever I think of this period in my life, I'm reminded of a song by the Mighty Sparrow, from his 1967 Calypso Album, "Sparrow At The Hilton" entitled *"Education a Must"*.

> *Children go to school and learn well*
> *Otherwise later on in life you will ketch real hell*
> *Without an education in your head*
> *Your whole life will be pure misery*
> *You better off dead*
> *For there is simply no room in this whole wide world*
> *For an uneducated little boy or girl.*

Sparrow went on to win the Calypso King of Kings Competition with that song in 1988, and thinking of music, one of the highlights of the senior school social calendar was the end of term talent show, which I always participated in and which became so popular, that I received a number of invitations to appear at other shows organized by Frank Norville and George of the C.Y.O. Harmonites at the Castries Parish Center Venue. They encouraged me to expand my horizons. Those were the years when the C.Y.O was vibrant not only as a sports, social and cultural club but the venue was in fact a melting pot for young and old, black and white, rich and poor, not just in the city but throughout the island. *"Golden Boy Dave"* as I was dubbed, become known for his crooning mellow voiced love ballads, fashioned after Britain's Cliff Richard and America's Ricky Nelson, Elvis Presley and Percy Sledge.

I soon gravitated to the big stage at Clarke's Cinema and The Castries Town Hall receiving encore after encore! Other sensations at the time were Denis James, Sandra Lorde- (Little Miss Blue), Johnny Romiel, Vanroy Charles, Patsy Cadet, Merriman Joseph, Terry Wilson, Cave Compton, The superbs, and Frank Norville, The beatniks and The Strollers among a host of others. Those were fantastic years when one really felt the support and camaraderie of our people both on and off the stage.

When I was about 15 or 16 years, I recall taking part in a talent show at Clarke's Cinema. The room was hot, very hot and the capacity crowd of maybe 800 gave me a standing ovation when I performed "Bachelor Boy" by Cliff Richard and the other may have been a Ricky Nelson song, *"Encore, Encore, Encore!"* they yelled. Also on stage that night was fellow artiste Denis James, as well as the scintillating youthful Rick Wayne doing a couple of gyrating Elvis covers and his British hit song "In My Imagination" Rick also got encores that night and was so impressed with our performances (Denis and I) that he took the microphone and publicly announced that he was going to ensure that both of us would receive recording contracts in England, because we were too good to remain in Saint Lucia and he was going to be working actively to make this a reality. At which point nearly all the people in pit, circle and box, all stood up and gave him thunderous applause.

I remember looking forward week after week, month after month to hear from Rick, in anticipation of becoming a singing sensation in England. Such were the thoughts of two teenagers, but we never heard back from him. Yes! We were both naive little boys with big dreams.

Subsequently I joined The Tru Tones as their main vocalist and toured with them to the USA, St. Croix, Dominica, St. Vincent and Barbados where they recorded their very first album; but my most memorable tour was at "Expo 69" in Grenada where *Chanteulle Sessenne Descartes* with an amazing, talented string band, performed *La Rose/La Marguerite* songs and Tru Tones led by child prodigy Boo Hinkson brought the house down in the presence of Grenada's Premier Eric Gairy…. That was an unforgettable moment and a shot in the arm for the indigenous music of the island.

After Senior School I was recruited by *Redhead* to teach at the R.C. Boys Primary where I remained for a two year period in Juniors 1 and 3; and like my primary school days it was a life learning experience rubbing shoulders with the likes of Mr. Jones Jn Baptiste, Mr. Joseph Andrew, Messrs Fowell, John, Small, Fenelon, Chalon, Pierre, Hippolyte and Finisterre and the several others whom I can't now recall. However, I saw teaching as just a stepping stone to a world of challenging but hopefully exciting years for me.

My stint at the Government Treasury was for several months where I was one of those responsible for checking and approving payment vouchers for Companies which the state owed, as well as for the hundreds of fortnightly paid workers who came to the small, hot area in droves, usually quite vociferous for their money. That job was, in the main, boring and uninspiring. I guess it just wasn't for me so whenever possible, I would sneak away upstairs to WIBS Castries, a sub-station of The Windward Islands Broadcasting Service headquartered in Grenada. Winston Hinkson who was the Programme Officer had already known of my interest in radio, as I had intimated that to him during rehearsal sessions of his brothers band in the Riverside Road area. Before long I was reading out the Jaycees Bingo numbers on weekdays and on Saturdays hosted *"DJ Date"* with Jeff Fedee which made us extremely popular with listeners and the so called social status crowd at the time.

The programme was from 8:00 p.m – 12 midnight. We spun all the dance music in that era - US, U.K., and the Dance Bands and Calypsonians of the Region. The second most popular show was the T.T.T. Show, (The Top 12 Tunes) broadcast Sundays at 7:00 p.m. Even if I say so myself, we rocked! The listeners loved it. Come to think of it they had no choice, as there were only two radio stations in Saint Lucia back then.

The station was located at the extreme right hand corner on the first floor of the old government building just off the House of Assembly Chambers. The transmitter was housed in a little room to the right just before entering the multi-task area, with a small newsroom a couple of corridors away.

The 500sq ft. cubicle had a broadcast area of just over 100sq ft, a circular microphone suspended by a black lead, run across the low florescent lit ceiling to the level of the duty announcer who sat facing towards it, at an extremely antiquated console measuring about 24x18 inches with small turntables on each side and left of the broadcast console were three huge, cumbersome looking metal reel to reel ferrograph tape recorders, usually in the pause mode, ready to be cranked up with programmes like "Magazine File", News Inserts, occasional commercials and live recordings of local bands and artistes. At the back of the announcer was the record library which consisted of numerous albums and 45 rpm records in those days; to the right of the console was a very small storage room with equipment under repair, recorders, mics, mic-stands, leads, power cords and other technical supplies.

In the very center of the room was Winston's desk with a couple of chairs, as the area doubled up as an office where he sat writing scripts, conducted meetings and answered the telephone. At the extreme corner to his right was a long bench which served as a sitting area for those who needed to consult with him or who were there to participate in a live interview.

When the Live mic switch came on, the old noisy air conditioned unit was immediately cut off with the announcer having to shout to those in the room very loudly Ok! Quiet, Quiet! I'm coming on! Everyone sort of froze, remaining as still and quiet as possible until the all clear was given…It really was quite a robotic and amusing experience. How announcers were able to maintain focus, concentrating on the task at hand amidst so many distractions, I really don't know and added to that, was Winston's incessant smoking which filled the entire room making inhaling almost unbearable.

I had already set my sights on a broadcasting career and since WIBS had no fulltime employment, I got a job as a radio announcer at RCI and joined Emelda Charles (Cool E) Vaughn Noel (The Bumble Bee) and Heather Pilgrim where programmes were presented in English for a few hours daily. Most of RCI programmes were broadcast in French with the target audience being the French Island of Martinique some 20 miles to the North of Saint Lucia. The French Programming came on mornings from

5:30 – 8:00 a.m., the English from 8:00 – 10:00, then French again from 10:00 a.m. – 2:00 p.m., English from 2:00 – 6:00 p.m. and then French Service again from 6:00 p.m. until close down. The French announcers who resided in Saint Lucia, were quite a lively lot and integrated themselves nicely into the Saint Lucian society.

The Request Programme then was one of the most popular at the station. I can still recall D-Day at Beane Field in Vieux Fort when we were able to broadcast a major governmental Agricultural, Manufacturing and Tourism Exhibition with huge emphasis on the potential for touristic development as well as the accommodation of international flights to that part of the island. We set up a Live booth there and looking back now it really was quite a broadcast feat under engineer Tom Foster with technical support from Peter Ephraim. Also of note was the ever popular Sunday Afternoon Programme hosted by Vaughn Noel "St. Lucia Talent on Parade" which ran for several seasons and gave local artistes the opportunity to really showcase their talent. Who could ever forget the "Live Wire Shows" with TG Fury, Jimmy Heavens, Mark Joseph and others in that era?

Then in early 1972, The WIBS sub stations management decided to go their separate ways and so WIBS Castries became Radio Saint Lucia and commenced full time programming from its cubby hole location in Government Buildings. I acquired a lot of broadcast skills from Winston Hinkson and Margaret Roberts-Steele who was seconded to us from Grenada from time to time. I recall having a slight lisp and problems pronouncing some words with three and four syllables which I knew I had to work at if I had to be good at my craft, and so I practiced day and night for months and went through a strict regiment of placing some pebbles in my mouth while still trying to be heard audibly "word for word" by my peers on the other side of the room. I wasn't even aware when I overcame that hurdle. It was Winston who remarked one evening when I had completed a Newscast that I seemed to have overcome the problem. He had been listening to me in his car and the Newscast was practically flawless. No need to mention here how grateful I was that I had overcome such a challenge which certainly proved to me at the impressionable age of 21 that nothing is impossible once you are focused and put your heart and mind to it.

I learnt the importance of Diction, Articulation, Pronunciation, Intonation Voice Modulation, how to read at a steady pace and to conduct interviews properly and how to present music programmes of every musical genre. I was the morning host for several years along with co-workers Lucella Blanchard, Winston Springer, Ernie Seon and Greg Regis (the News Team) with Ben Carter and Harold George the technicians.

Those were amazing years indeed when Radio Saint Lucia aired some edifying programmes. I particularly remember Carnival which was a pre Lenten festival in those days and my going to Trinidad to interview Sparrow and Kitchener in 1975, and producing a Stella Programme "Road March Hits 1963-1975" or "The Reverence of Christmas" and the incredible thought provoking interviews and discussions with local and regional politicians and public servants. There were a lot of human interest stories produced by Winston Hinkson, Lucella Blanchard, and myself.

All of this was a labor of love so you would really understand my amusement when present day announcers speak of not being able to produce much due to inadequate space and lack of the most technologically advanced equipment….we did a lot in those days with less! It really was quite a feat in team-work and broadcasting excellence.

To quote Jerry George: "As with many broadcasters of that period, Samuels learned to be a 'master of all' to rock the listening audience with fast-paced drive time music shows, then to present the news with the seriousness and authority the job demanded. He also hosted classical music shows and outside broadcasts, all with the finesse of the true professional. This was at a time, unlike today, when proper diction, pronunciation and articulation mattered. As for the sound of his voice, it remains to this day distinguished for its special clarity and tone".

I spent four years at RSL as a radio announcer 1972-76. Then I was fired along with Winston Springer and Ernie Seon. I was being seen in official circles as a militant and was playing a lot of anti-establishment songs on the radio. It was a time of great political change in the country and in the region with a dose of radicalism that seemed to have affected every single island.

In Trinidad in 1970, there was a Black power revolution the seeds of which quickly spread. Groups advocating Black Power surfaced everywhere and Saint Lucia was no exception with George Odlum, Peter Josie and others stepping forward to challenge the status quo. In the 1974 election run up I was leaning towards Odlum and Josie and the music I was playing on air left no doubt where my political loyalties lay. I just knew I was heading into hot water. The move towards unionization by RSL employees in which I was deeply involved, came at the same time and must have presented the perfect opportunity to discipline me. We employees of RSL felt that we were being left behind and that the management of the quasi government station was not doing enough for us, that our terms and conditions left a lot to be desired. We were branded as "rebels". I remember very well receiving my letter of dismissal. One evening I was at home and the letter was delivered signed by Winston Hinkson, obviously on the instructions of the Cabinet, firing us with immediate effect.

So my world collapsed that evening. Broadcasting was all that I had done from my late teens. I wondered what next. I wasn't sure for a while. Jeff by then had moved on to Radio Antilles. (Big A) on the island of Montserrat. The station which was owned by German Radio Corporation "Dutshe Welle" was heard on 930 a.m. and, boasted of 100,000 watts of power. It was arguably the most listened to station throughout the entire Eastern Caribbean. Jeff hosted the morning programme but it was Drive Time from 3-6pm that made him a household name in the region. Having been made aware of my situation, he invited me over for a visit. I went On Air with him a few times as we explored job prospects there. The Montserrat authorities were by then aware of broadcasters in the sub region seeking jobs at Big A and made the work permit process difficult. There was the feeling too that priority was being given to Montserrat nationals and the other leeward islanders. So it was with disappointment and some uncertainty about my future, that I returned to Saint Lucia after six weeks stay in that island.

Meanwhile the Tru Tones, now an orchestra, was still the island's leading dance band, even though fans of the competing Quavers would argue differently. Both bands would stage regular performances at popular dance spots Palm Beach and Camelot- a stone's throw away and because of my broadcasting ability, I was recruited by them to present a series of packaged floor shows at some major hotels in the Castries basin. As a result of that exposure and the success of these shows to the hotel guests, I was offered the post of Social Director at the Halcyon Beach Club managed by Caribbean Hotel Management Services (CHMS). Within months I was promoted to PR and Entertainment Director of all their properties.... Halcyon Sands at Vigie, Halcyon Days in Vieux Fort and The Saint Lucian at Rodney Bay.

During that period 1977-1980, I also presented a weekly tourism programme on radio "Halcyon Quarter" which served to inform the public about the importance and benefits to be derived from that major industry, interviewing everyone from vendor to taxi driver, hotel owner to restaurant owner and tourism executive to Government Ministers and officials. Apart from raising the profile of the CHMS Group, I also set about hiring, exposing and improving the opportunities for entertainers within the hotel chain.

One of the biggest entertainment events to ever be staged in Saint Lucia was "STOP" At Halcyon" where we constructed a stage over the swimming pool in the very center of the beach club, before a capacity crowd of over 1000 people. The event featured the *crème de la crème* of Saint Lucian talent. Many musicians and artistes concur that there was something magical and spectacular about that era...a great deal was done by the CHMS group to really open its doors and make Saint Lucians feel welcome at all times. The Fisherman's Wharf at HBC was known as the entertainment capital in Castries while Halcyon Days Hotel (HDH) was the same for the southern area. I appreciated and respected my employers, Bill Stewart and Theo Gobat as they did everything to provide a conducive working environment for me and I compensated by providing the best PR for the group not only in Saint Lucia but in the travel trade magazines in Europe and North America, which I believe was responsible for The Halcyon

Beach Club being the chosen venue for The Formal Independence State Dinner attended by Prime Minister John Compton and Mrs. Compton and dignitaries from here, the region and the world including Britain's Princess Alexandra and husband who represented Queen Elizabeth 11, who were all here to participate in the festivities to mark Saint Lucia's attainment of Independence from Britain, just hours before the lowering of the Union Jack and the hoisting of the Saint Lucia Flag for the first time as an independent Saint Lucia. It was an awesome patriotic display by HBC management. I had never seen the hotel look so beautiful, bedecked in the colors of the national flag.

Meanwhile, a few weeks later, I was instructed by the company to ensure the success of a new discothèque at the Saint Lucian, and despite my opposition, they decided to name it Lucifer's. I was responsible for everything to do with the hype and the launch of the disco with a big cocktail party at which the 'Who's who' in the island were present.

Those who conceptualized the theme in England, as if the name was not controversial enough, decided to place the numbers 666 on the dance floor. Patrons sat in a cone-like structure a little away from the dance area; against the 4 walls were huge crater-like stone images in black with red lights at the back to give the effect of blazing volcanic activity or maybe the attempt was to give a feel of what hell must be like. I was extremely uncomfortable about this, but there was nothing I could have done about it. In many ways this move really crystallized the lack of spirituality in human kind, that we would be so driven in advancing the cause of making money by any means necessary, at the risk of negating a relationship with God and in the process fall in the trap of the dark, wicked spiritual forces in space that seek to control we mortals here on earth.

CHAPTER 3

CUNARD BYTES

"Life shouldn't be just carnal, but spiritual."

If the decade of the 50s was one of social and political change, the 60's and 70's saw the island's cultural advancement and sheer excitement in many forms. Internationally, the space race between the United States and the Soviet Union that had started in the previous decade reached new intensity. The Kennedys commanded the spotlight in U.S. politics and Martin Luther King stepped up the civil rights struggle. In sport, the West Indies began their ascendancy in world cricket following their historic test series (which they lost 2-1) in Australia that included the first ever tied match.

That period also unleashed a revolution in popular music dominated by Britain's Beatles and Rolling Stones, The Beach Boys, the Doors and Soul music in the United States. In the Caribbean, the era of great dance bands like the Dutchy Brothers, Joey Lewis, Ron Berridge Orchestras of Trinidad and Tobago, Byron Lee and the Dragoneers, the Blues Busters and the Ska and Rock Steady Movement of Jamaica, which later mushroomed into the internationally acclaimed Reggae Dance beat and the Bob Marley and the Wailers Revolution.

Barbados created a music beat called "Spouge" which was marketed and distributed throughout the region by a company called West Indies Records Ltd, (WIRL) which produced records from artistes from the

Caribbean. Some of the big names were Emile Straker and the Merrymen, the Sand Pebbles and a host of male and female artistes including Wendy Allyne, Fern Trail, Jackie Opel, Richard Stoute, the Draytons Two and from Guyana Johnny Braff and Mark Holder, including our very own Emile Ford, Patsy Cadet, Denis James, the Mighty Pelay with the Big Six Orchestra, along with other popular local bands like the Tru Tones, Quavers and Vibratones. Women's Lib, Flower Power (Hippie Movement) and the shortening of skirt lengths, popularly known as the "mini skirt" was the fashion trend of the day. In the Caribbean, an attempt to federate the English speaking islands disappointingly floundered in 1962; but initiatives towards regional integration were actually stepped up.

In Saint Lucia, a change in government ushered in more dynamic leadership and a different kind of revolution that drastically changed the social and economic landscape. It brought Saint Lucia into the age of modernization with the introduction of pipe borne water in some homes, an automatic telephone system, expansion of electricity and television among other novelties.

It was also the period when Saint Lucia began to seriously launch its bid to become a tourism destination with a massive investment in tourism plant – Cariblue Hotel and Saint Lucia Beach Hotel in the North, Halcyon Beach Club at Choc, Malabar and Blue Waters Hotels at Vigie and Villa Hotel and San Antoine in the City and Halcyon Days Hotel in Vieux Fort. The banana boom also provided farmers with the opportunity for prosperity and progress, as we witnessed major infrastructural developments taking place especially in the northwest cauldron of the island.

Then on August 3rd, 1980, disaster struck Saint Lucia in very much the same way that Hurricane David dealt a severe blow to sister island Dominica a year earlier. Hurricane Allen had unleashed its fury. Several of the islands hotels were extensively damaged, the agricultural sector and in particular the Banana Industry were completely wiped out. Schools, Hospitals, Health Centers, Sporting facilities, domestic dwellings including Bridges, Roads, Electricity, Water and other infrastructural assets were not spared the intensity of the elements. I recall spending the entire time (some 6 hours) in my apartment bathroom, on the toilet seat, as it seemed like the safest place to be, listening to the intensity and howling of the wind and the heavy pounding of the rain on the roof which made a loud creaking sound. What an agonizingly long moment that was. It was truly a miracle that the roof remained intact. I will never understand how so many of us survived Hurricane Allen.

Added to the passage of Hurricane Allen was the political uncertainty in the island with the resignation of two Prime Ministers within the space of one year and the emergence of an Interim Government for a period of a few months. Clearly the challenges were immense for the commercial sector, the security forces and for the people of Saint Lucia. During that same period, it was not unusual to hear some animated discussion about Grenada's Revolutionary Government and its charismatic Prime Minister Maurice Bishop, who had ousted the eccentric Eric Gairy in a bloodless Coup. Obviously, there was grave concern being expressed at home, the diaspora and from friendly Governments in the region and internationally, that Saint Lucia may have been heading along the same revolutionary path as Grenada. Fortunately, it was not to be.

Sometime during the early part of 1982, I arrived at my CDC flat on High Street and noted that there were a number of messages awaiting me on my answering machine. There was one in particular which peaked my curiosity as it was the coarse, unique but familiar German voice of Mr. Alex Oostenbrink, the General Manager of Cunard La Toc Hotel and La Toc Suites, where I had emceed on behalf of the Tru Tones fortnightly Cabaret shows. He had often been very cordial engaging me in several discourses on tourism, politics and other pertinent events of the day over a round of drinks. I phoned him and we spoke for a while and he asked me if I could come to the hotel to see him as soon as possible. I obliged a day or so later and one week after the call, I was appointed the hotel's Guest Relations Manager with responsibility for enhancing the entertainment, improving the information and tours desk with the goal of generating more interest in guests undertaking more excursion tours of the island, neighboring Martinique and the Grenadine Islands and which would redound to more sales and earnings for the resort. I was also to ensure that there were fewer disgruntled guests and that many of the hotel happenings were disseminated to the local press and travel trade magazines in the UK and USA.

Cunard La Toc Resort was a 100 acre property with 158 rooms all with a view of the ocean; there were 60 one and two bedroom suites some with a private plunge pool, and just south of the main hotel, 100 units some of which were luxury suites with a plunge pool. The property boasted of three main restaurants and four bars. However, just before starting my stint, I was given a one week cruise on board one of the company's cruise ships, "Cunard Countess" which would berth at port Castries weekly. I still recall the facial expression of one of the ship's agents when the time came to depart and he asked me what I was still doing on board the ship despite the announcements. He was at a loss for words when I told him why I was on board: that it was all part of an orientation exercise to prepare me for the job at the hotel. It was one of the most pleasurable experiences I've ever had and the Cruise Director and staff pulled out all the stops to give me a really great time....I felt like Cinderfella...we went as far as St. Thomas in the north, Venezuela down south and back up across Barbados in the East.

I reported to work one week later, towards the end of September, 1982, and immediately set about carrying out the mandate given to me. I contracted a number of groups like Survival Band with Mervyn Wilkinson and Jennifer Gaston, Eric Adley's and Rameau Poleon's Mount Gallion group from V-Fort, Caribbean Rockers and Diamond Steel among others as well as solo artistes from around the island.....The floor shows and entertainment at La Toc began to get a lot of attention and Saint Lucians and visitors from other hotels turned out in fairly large numbers to be part of the Tuesday and Saturday evening events in particular. The hotel also laid out a variety of culinary delights to excite the taste buds of visiting patrons.

A highlight of the Cunard tourist experience was a visit to the Green Parrot Restaurant. There were no All Inclusives in those days and we would "Pack da place up" with hundreds of tourists weekly. The most popular dining experience was "Ladies Free Night" -- Ladies wearing a flower in their hair and accompanied by a gentleman were entitled to a FREE dinner – It was an evening of formal and elegant attire; Wednesdays and Saturdays were Caribbean and International Show Nights preceded by a generous sampling of "*Juk Fu Yea Soup*", "Stuffed Pussy Entrée" (avocado with farine and saltfish) and other gastronomic delights too numerous to mention here, all complimented by Chef's amazing multi-talented antics, whether it was Fire eating, Belly Dancing, Limbo Dancing with Princesses Venus and Tina, Sexy Rex's Bicycle Stunts, The Snake Man, The Dance Troupe-Lightning Stars and the indefatigable, ever faithful musicians – Tropical Stars … but there's more!

Chef's Booming Operatic vocals were not just spectacular but invoked hilarious glee especially when he sang the patriotic songs of The UK, Germany, France, Italy and Spain (in their languages) USA, Canada, Australia and even West Indians got a special vocal treat which ended up with Chef leading a conga line dance through the restaurant lounge and patio… the sound of mirth and music resounded all over Morne Fortune. Even the city wasn't spared the infectious rhythms from late nights, into the wee hours of the morning… How many of us recall his special birthday and anniversary tributes with restaurant and kitchen staff carrying cake with lighted candles to a surprised group at table. Whenever we wanted to impress family, friends and visitors, we knew that "Satisfaction was always guaranteed at the Green Parrot" Remember those New Years Eve Dinners with impressive fireworks displays? Those were tremendously wonderful days; Yes! The Green Parrot was a must go to – Saint Lucian Hospitality personified!

I had a really good Cunard team that comprised Camilla, Agatha, Canice, David, Ronnie and Bert the DJ. After some three years, Alex Oostenbrink was succeeded by Englishman Peter Sylvester and at the time of my leaving, the man at the helm was Michael Marco an American of Middle East extraction. About a year or so later the hotel closed down and was purchased by Sandals Resorts International who spent millions to transform the original property, including the construction of a massive swimming pool along the area where the terrace and bandstand used to be. I love what Sandals have done but there was something quite special and classy about Cunard La Toc that I have not seen at any other hotel plant up to this day. That period of my life was gratifying. I became skilled in events management which made me grow in confidence because of the exposure to guests from all over the world and the manner they went about "Affirming" my staff and me. There were also many opportunities to undertake excursions to neighboring islands, regular trips on board the Cunard ships and the QE11, which would be anchored imposingly at the front of the hotel, as it was too large a vessel to enter the Castries Harbour. It really was a camera-man's delight and I dare say it must have been the same for both the hotel guests and the passengers on board.

My day usually started at about 9:00 am until 4:00 p.m, but I was usually back at 6:30 to mingle with guests, sometimes, host the cocktail party and then after dinner, present the evening's entertainment. Usually I left for home about 11pm. Sundays were usually my day off which I would spend driving around exploring Saint Lucia and visited The Canai's, Lubins, Biscette and Jn Baptiste families of Micoud, Winall and Christine Joshua and The Valmont's and Maxwell's of Vieux Fort and the Gustave Family of Soufriere. Up to this day most of the above are like family...I love and cherish them all dearly. For me the Sunday drive to the countryside, and taking in the lush green vegetation and topography of the island through quaint villages and towns with the friendliest people in this hemisphere, was and still is nothing short of therapeutic.

While at La Toc, I recognized that enough wasn't being done to market and advertise the island as a tourist destination so I endeavored to acquire the training and skills required in the production of maps and videography; I got to meet Andrew Hulsmeier, one of Barbados' leading Still Photographers and Videographers who had produced a 30 minute video on Barbados and I thought that I could commission him to produce a Saint Lucia Video for me. I also met Stuart Jenkins, a sort of eccentric Barbados based Briton and a saxophonist with a passion for jazz, who engineered and supported the production of a "Sky view" map of Saint Lucia - which he skillfully charted himself- a three dimensional aerial perspective of the island, similar to a series of them he had done for Barbados and the rest of the islands in this archipelago. The map was a tremendous success and within a couple of years a smaller folded version was produced which served as a very handy tool for the visitor undertaking excursions of the island. The large original map printed in England was launched at Cunard La Toc in the presence of Prime Minister Compton, Tourism Minister George Mallet, Tourism Director Egbert Mathurin and a broad section of Governmental, Tourism and business officials in Saint Lucia. I was able to attract nearly one hundred clients who purchased advertising space of various sizes on the map, so it was quite an economically viable project.

Some of the best Christmas' I've had have been spent at Cunard La Toc; it's funny as I think back, but as a department we all had to show up and chip in at work to ensure that "Our Guests" were given a great time and that was not easy being away from our families and in a sense being with "Our Cunard Family". Yet, we enjoyed those moments immensely, the highlight being Christmas Day and New Years' Eve of course!

For days on end my staff was engaged in assisting with the putting up of the Christmas trees, holly and decorations, not only in the main hotel lobby but over at the village, TV room, restaurants, bars and anywhere that was an assembly point for our guests. The kitchen and bar staff went overboard in creating some amazing culinary and exotic bar delights and because it was Christmas, there was usually a very high percentage of families and lots of children, which meant that their participation in hotel outdoor activities was taken to a level not experienced at any other time of the year.

On Christmas day at approximately 10am, Santa arrived by sea on skis, by boat, horse drawn buggy and one year, instead of Santa, we announced that due to illness he was unable to visit, but Mrs. Santa would appear instead. Hundreds of guests with their cameras ready were waiting to capture that special moment to pose with Santa or Mrs. Santa….What a wonderful moment that was especially for the young kids. Many of the parents lost some self-control by drinking too much during the day and as a result, failed to make it to the lavish entertainment put on for them in the evening on the terrace bandstand.

However, nothing the hotel planned during the year was anything like the New Years Eve Dinner, the marvelous musical entertainment on display, the countdown and in anticipation, the sound of champagne bottles popping all over the place and the always incredible fireworks display that usually took an entire day to set up on the beach right in front of the property and the dancing and partying that went on until daybreak; Oh what a night! I do believe that many of us lived for that one moment in our hotel life. I don't have to tell you how difficult it was for us to return to Cunard La Toc later that morning sort of zombie like, but if there was any consolation, it is that we weren't the only ones.

Meanwhile at Cunard, we started a project where we would give visitors the opportunity to actually wine and dine at Saint Lucian homes so that they could experience the true hospitality of our people. Also when the Cunard Countess docked weekly at the ports, some hotel employees and entertainers were able to be part of an exchange programme between the hotel resort and the ship.

RCI/Splash

During my Cunard stint, I found time to assist in the setting up of RCI's 101.1 FM Service. The radio station had been broadcasting on 840AM for nearly three decades, first at Vigie and later downtown Castries on the top floor of the Saint Lucia Agriculturist's Association building behind the First Caribbean Bank on Bridge Street. I spent a couple of years there and hosted music programmes on Tuesday and Thursday afternoons and was responsible for introducing a few youngsters to the broadcast profession.

Around that same period, I was approached by Lawrence Samuel, General Manager of The Saint Lucian Hotel, to manage Splash Night Club which had replaced Lucifer's as one of the prime night spots in the north of the island. Lucifer's was razed to the ground by a mystery fire a few months before. After a couple of years, I began feeling that the night life was taking it's toll. Besides I thought that I was stretching myself a bit too thin and added to that there were beginning to be some questions raised at the hotel about my loyalty to Cunard, so I contracted an acquaintance of mine of many years to supervise the operation of the night club for me, but would visit regularly to ascertain that all was well. Splash was extremely successful during that era.

One of the many things which impacted me and still does to this day, is driving through Castries along the La Toc road in front of faux-a-chaux and encountering the slum like housing that greets you as you drive by with the waterfront and the former Geest banana shed turned partly ferry terminal on your immediate right; more of that type of housing is in full view all along the way, as you meander up the hill around the corner with the old Golden Hope main office block to your right....then at a certain point you are at a level to take in the panoramic view of Castries City with its Miami styled waterfront and the government buildings dotting the landscape in the background with the harbor in the foreground. What a delightful sight! Particularly when there are four cruise ships in port. Just a little bit further a right turn leads you into the quarter mile entrance of Cunard La Toc turned Sandals.

The sloping lush greens and manicured grounds beckon with all the flora imaginable, revealing the 9 hole golf course and rising above it, the beautiful homes on the hillside of Coubaril; it was like coming from a Saint Lucian reality into a fantasy land-and now many years later when driving to Sandals, I still get that same extraordinary feeling that not much has changed. Clearly there needs to be some political will to enhance the waterfront which would necessitate the moving of the numerous container trucks parked haphazardly and including the slum-like dwellings and their occupants, who have lived in those areas for many decades.

The interesting thing about my years with Cunard was that they pointed out to me the possibilities that existed in the tourism sector for anyone with imagination and drive. I considered I had both and so it was that I decided that the time had come to go into my own business.

CHAPTER 4

THE GLORY YEARS

"Economic Growth is bound to be slow unless there is an
adequate supply of entrepreneurs looking out for new ideas,
and willing to take the risk of introducing them."
(Sir Arthur Lewis Dictum– Noble Laureate for Economics – 1979)

Saint Lucia's attainment of Independence in 1979 created a new dynamism among young people on the island. I remember the arguments during the years of the pre-independence discussions, with some expressing fears that the island would not be able to stand on its own feet and was heading into turbulent waters by breaking away fully from the "mother country". Few gave any recognition to the fact that Saint Lucia had, in fact, been doing just that since March 1967 when the British gave the island Associated Statehood and with it the right to chart our own domestic affairs. Britain kept responsibility for our defense and external relations, for obvious reasons, but from Statehood, we began to decide for ourselves how our government should function, who we should appoint where, what kind of development we wanted to pursue and where our national priorities lay. I am not sure whether it was my confidence in the political leadership we had at that time or the desire for my own independence, given the circumstances of my early years growing up virtually on my own but I got to the stage where I was being bitten by a bug to move out and chart my own destiny as well. Many other young men and women of my age were similarly bitten with the result that a new generation of young business people was beginning to emerge.

Saint Lucia underwent a period of political uncertainty in the three years immediately following Independence with infighting within the newly elected Saint Lucia Labour Party government but once it was peacefully resolved in mid 1982 with new elections, the island began to breathe freely again, putting to rest claims that we did not have the capacity to handle our own internal affairs. By the middle of the decade, Saint Lucia was beginning to move forward again. Both bananas and tourism were flourishing as was the manufacturing sector. It was the right time for enterprising young persons to stamp their mark, so I promptly took the plunge. I had gained experience in the broadcasting field and then used that talent in the tourism sector. Now I was ready to marry the two into an entirely new venture: David Samuels Promotions and Video Productions Limited (DSP), a public relations and advertising company.

You see while at CHMS and Cunard, I had developed confidence in myself and in my own ability that I had not demonstrated in all my years in radio. I found that as a radio announcer my self- esteem had been somewhat at a low ebb. I was not sure of who and what I was. However, at these hotel chains, I had received a lot of rave reviews from guests based on my interaction with them and the way I had been able to assist in making their stay in Saint Lucia rewarding and enjoyable. I started to think that, with the right moves, I could go into a new direction that had even greater potential, I realized that I was a good spokesman for Saint Lucia.

Just how did DSP get off the ground? There was this friend of mine, Andrew Hulsmeier of Barbados who had a video production facility. He suggested to me that from time to time we could both make a little money. If I had anyone in Saint Lucia who needed TV commercials produced he would come to Saint Lucia to do the filming, then go back to Barbados to edit. We did some work together but I soon discovered the need to establish my own facility because of a few niggling problems I had not anticipated. Thus, I launched DSP. On other previous occasions whenever I had sought to do something, I always got a lot of negative responses that it would not work for this or that reason. That bugged me. To this day I have never been able to understand why is it that, when a Saint Lucian sets out to do something different, he is always being told that it will not work, it will not succeed. I decided to ignore the negativity and take all the skills that I had acquired in broadcasting into this new venture. I felt that I had done as much as could be done at Cunard.

In 1988, DSP started off with one camera and what were some domestic pieces that I'd purchased from some guy who was folding up. Then a few months later I purchased a Umatic editing suite and an additional camera. During a function at Cunard La Toc to commemorate the 10 Anniversary of Saint Lucia's Independence and in the presence of PM Compton and other government and tourism officials, I had the opportunity to virtually introduce and promote DSP as it were, with the official launch of the video, Images of Saint Lucia, the Skyview Map and the Rameau Poleon Album "Sweet Sounds of Saint Lucia."

Here is an extract of my address: "We run a company whose principal aim is to hold up the mirror of things Saint Lucian. For me this is a convenient vehicle for expressing a consuming love for my country. In our commitment to this land that gave us birth, we are determined that Saint Lucia should not waste its sweetness on the dessert air. We will describe it, we will portray it, and we will preserve its rhythms and extol its beauty. We will depict its history; we will expose its charms and we will elevate its people."

In his response, Prime Minister Compton said, "New Saint Lucians are emerging, new Saint Lucians are taking the opportunities that are available to them., not sitting back, crying and waiting for things to happen but rather they are causing things to happen. We see young Saint Lucians all around doing extraordinary things. That is what gives us hope and gives me the satisfaction of the decision we took 10 years ago to become an independent country – to remove from our soul this dead hand of colonialism that makes us denigrate ourselves, making us feel like we are second class citizens in the world, some people who cannot rule themselves, who cannot govern themselves – and knowing the horizon of tomorrow is open to us, all of us who dare, all of us who have the ambition, who have the drive, can take the opportunities that are now available to bring Saint Lucia into the forefront of things in the Caribbean. It is young people, young entrepreneurs like Dave, who have the opportunity and are prepared to grasp it, take the risks and move this country forward. "And Dave – let me congratulate you and the young people of Saint Lucia who've done so much over the last 10 years to make us proud, and as we look into the mirror that Dave has produced, we see a thriving, a vibrant and above all a beautiful people." (*P.M. Compton at the 10th Independence Anniversary Function in the presence of George Mallet, Louis George, other Government and Tourism Officials, including specially invited guests*).

By 1993 we gravitated to a Sony Beta Editing Suite complimented with Sony Beta Cameras. We very quickly established ourselves as the leading facility in Saint Lucia and one of the leaders in the Organization of Eastern Caribbean States (O.E.C.S.), as we were on the cutting edge of video technology.

At DSP, one of the first things I did was to start a television series, TOURISM IS OUR BUSINESS, which went on for several years. I used the same sort of approach as I had done with HALCYON QUARTER because it was aimed at enlightening Saint Lucians about tourism and seeking their support for the industry. I really enjoyed that, because up to this day, I have always felt that our people have not been given enough reason to embrace tourism. I hold the view that more needs to be done by the authorities to get Saint Lucians to accept tourism. Many people that I still speak with, make the point about the importance of the industry, but sadly, there is still a lot of suspicion among the population about the industry and how much Saint Lucia is really benefiting from it. So DSP produced "Fun in Paradise," a shorter video, unlike the documentary approach of the earlier production. It really mirrored the country as a fun place to be and was available at several shops and boutiques, especially at hotels.

The friendships forged with these Barbadian contacts were deeply rewarding in innumerable ways and the professionalism exemplified was unlike anything I had experienced in Saint Lucia. They were truly really class acts. The same can be said of Keith and Sally Miller from Barbados who collaborated with us in producing, "Saint Lucia in your Pocket", a high quality pocket guide with a fold out map that was produced twice yearly and which was aimed at all visitors and distributed at major hotels, tour operators and all tourist outlets in the country. The publication hit the market in 1995 and 1996

Wrote Jerry George, in a newspaper article later: "The map and booklet were the first of their kind in Saint Lucian advertising history. You could say Samuels was ahead of his time but it was thanks to his efforts that many Saint Lucians got their start in the field of video production. Some went on to establish their own companies. Samuels and DSP occupied the advertising spotlight for use of E-BON . . . then used as the tag line for a Piton beer ad. The phrase remains in popular use by Saint Lucians for anything regarded as superlatively wonderful."

DSP also quickly established itself as Saint Lucia's first record production company. In 1988 we produced the album, WOY, which featured some of the top calypsonians at the time, like Pep, Educator, Tricky, Short Pants, Invader, General Kneah and Chippy. WOY was a collaboration with Clarence Joseph, arranger, and Boo Hinkson, with Recording Engineer Norman Barrow of Barbados actually coming to Saint Lucia with all his recording equipment and accessories to work on the project: Then there was "Sweet Sounds of Saint Lucia, featuring 'Rameau' Joseph Poleon and band, which earned DSP an M&C Fine Arts award in 1989. Also the music album "The King, The Dread and Buffalo", a tribute to Ashanti, Herb Black and Buffalo in 1991. All of these were landmark projects because no one else was doing them.

I was told that a video on Saint Lucia would not sell but DSP went on to produce two. Also people would not support shacshac music, and so when I produced Rameau Poleon, the gifted violinist and his band, few gave this venture any chance of success. It was a bold, creative and innovative musical gem which was recorded by Eli Louis in Studio 4 at Radio Saint Lucia...

This project encouraged me to venture into record production and show promotions and so, in a span of seven years, we were able to invite Kassav, Jimmy Cliff in 1991, Relator and Sparrow at least three times... We never made a profit but just about broke even. It appeared as though everyone made money except us. Those were the days when you had to invest at least $15,000 for stage construction, $7,000 for Sound System, $5,000 for lighting, $3,000.00 for Security and of course artistes fees, accommodation and transportation. There were always issues with ticket sales at the entrance, which made it difficult to make a profit and besides, scores, if not hundreds, were able to undermine the security system and gain free entry into the Mindoo Philip Park.

Staging Shows is tough and I learnt a lot...you might say "the hard way". All of those efforts though, would not have been possible without the sponsorship of companies like WLBL, Du Boulay's Bottling, KFC and Saint Lucia Distillers among others.

But DSP also came face to face with petty island politics and there were some who were not prepared to forget my association with the Socialist Leaning Odlum, so much so that I incurred the wrath of a couple of government officials. I also needed duty free concession to start up DSP as I wanted to import thousands of dollars' worth of new equipment into the country. George Odlum actually helped me prepare the papers for submission to the Cabinet of Ministers. I was told that a couple members of the government then had attempted to block me. However, they were overruled by Prime Minister John Compton who made the point that I was a Saint Lucian and further, that my venture had the potential for growing the economy. I got the concessions for 10 years and the way some people saw it, I was moving too fast and in the process, I was seen as a threat to some who were then dominating certain sections of the economy, especially in the tourism sector. After all, my company's services were being sought not only in Saint Lucia but also as far south as Trinidad and as far north as Antigua and we were really sailing high.

As a young, black Saint Lucian business owner, I confronted all forms of discrimination, particularly in the race and social status sphere, but at times it was very subtle, especially when dealing with white owned or white managed businesses. I always felt that I had to work so much harder and produce so much more professionally to get the contracts, thousands of dollars less than what they'd have to pay to Trinidadian and Barbadian companies. It was something my inner circle at DSP could not, or would not have understood and which I never shared with them, due to a sort of naiveté that was generally part of their modus operandi.

Most of the time we were inundated with so much work, that I had to contract certain business associates to assist in the scripting and narration of documentaries and infomercials, and it was always a great sense of bother even when I had discussions with those very same persons 4-6 weeks in advance, that they wouldn't begin to commence work on the project until some 2-3 days before the official presentation to the customers. I don't know if it had something to do with their general lack of appreciation for time lines or it may have been a deliberate move on their part 'To have me wait'. It was all very sad and unprofessional and created a lot of unnecessary stress and jarred nerves. Some of those people; friends, associates, acquaintances who demonstrated external support, were privately harboring a lot of grouses and negativity towards me and my businesses. Those were tough times and diminished a lot of enthusiasm and zeal for my work. I learned much!

Another thing was the lack of appreciation for "Excellence" or working hard towards its attainment. You would more often hear *'Man! Da thing good like dat!'*, when I would have preferred 'I think we should change this or include that to make it better' Such are the challenges that a young black person confronts in the competitive, hostile business environment of Saint Lucia and that is where my faith helped. Some have described me as being fussy, which would motivate me to push myself even more, so I viewed that characterization as a compliment-dotting the I's and crossing the T's, as if there was something wrong with that? Where I drew the line however is when they made it seem that I was acting as though I was better than them and everyone else. I've always viewed that comment as woefully unfortunate and unfair, as I've never considered myself better than anyone else and never will....It's just not who and what I am.

I've always relied on criticism to fuel my passions, but I've noticed that a vast number of our people simply would not take kindly to any form of it for a number of reasons. Only recently I was watching EWTN and the priest was reading from the Gospel of Matthew, which speaks to the beauty, majesty, mercy and forgiveness of God. The fact that I have friends and acquaintances who have various forms of addictions and may even be thieves, liars and cheats, does not prevent me 'A Sinner' from offering them advice or admonishing them for their wrong doings, It doesn't make me feel that I am better or saintly, but I would have failed in my Christian duty, if I had not confronted them with their personal challenges, but I reiterate, it does not in any way mean that I am, or feel better than them.

Everything changed when I decided to build my home and DSP Studios at the Morne. Putting up the structure seemed to have troubled a lot of people and a host of bizarre things started happening. The evidence is there. We had shot up to become the number one video production company in the country, if not in the OECS and I had with me right up to the end, the talented Anius team, Fimbar and Johnny, who were sometimes joined by Johnny's brother Thomas.

Fimbar headed the production facility and for the first few years, I brought in Sony experts in various aspects of the field to train our staff. Fimbar was assisted by Johnny, Thomas chipped in whenever there were busy periods and Dinesh spent a couple of years with us. Both Fimbar and Johnny had come over from HTS which was located just up the hill from our Morne studios. I want to place on record my grateful thanks to Fimbar (who passed in 2016) his family, Johnny and family, and all those who were a part of this dynamic company, for enriching my life so much. I know that when I insisted on excellence, some of you did not initially understand and thought that I was being difficult and unappreciative, but in due course, especially when you moved out on your own, you quickly recognized that we live in a global village and only persons who are hard working and committed to excellence, and are uncompromising when it comes to quality, will succeed and carve a niche in this competitive environment.

DSP rapidly gained regional recognition, so much so, we were able to attract the attention of international agencies like UNESCO and OAS, through their regional offices as well as the OECS Secretariat, Sir Arthur Lewis Community College, Saint Lucia Tourist Board and a couple of Multi-National companies with headquarters in Saint Lucia. Most of these clients for many years provided satisfactory financial returns for my company.

Also in 1996, the John Compton Cabinet of Ministers approved the granting of a broadcast license to DSP to open an FM Radio Station, but due to the liberalization of the broadcast sector, and the multiplicity of radio stations since 2001, I have been somewhat reluctant to open up such a service, although I am optimistic that my programme format would probably be a most novel and welcome concept in the Saint Lucian broadcast environment.

Around that same time I also opened up a CD music shop called SIGHTS AND SOUNDS with the main store at Gablewoods Mall and a smaller branch on Micoud Street.

All the while, however, storm clouds were hovering overhead and I was being set up for the fall, but I did not know it.

CHAPTER 5

THE "JOB" MAN

"Storms have a purpose from God's perspective."

The world was changing rapidly as the decade of the nineties dawned, but for developing countries like Saint Lucia, it was not a change for the better. The vital banana industry that had created a social and economic revolution in the previous two decades was in declining mode, and its foundations began to tremble. Production costs had escalated, forcing farmers out of the industry in droves. However, when the preferential access to the British market that Saint Lucia had enjoyed for years came under threat in an era that was being termed "globalization," the bottom of the industry began to cave in. Growers began to call for less government and more grower control of the industry. They also began to agitate for a greater share of the returns from the industry. The protestors adopted a posture of militancy that exploded in violence on the farms and physical confrontation on the streets. Banana production dropped, the national economy came under pressure, businesses began to suffer and competition became fierce. It was then that a series of totally bizarre things began to occur at DSP.

One day I was having a discussion with Fr. Stephen Quinlan (Fr. Q) at The Castries Cathedral about the strange experiences that I had been encountering at my businesses. I explained that there were times when the days' earnings were extremely encouraging, but those gains just seemed to vanish, much to my surprise, he asked me, "Is it like your pocket is full, but it has a hole, and before long its contents are emptied?" "Yes!" I replied. Fr. Q continued, "Do you know anything about occultism?" I didn't know about it and I told him so. He tried to explain it all to me. It was at the time that the construction of my home/business complex was taking place, and very much at the foundation stage. There were many issues with the construction works which were exacerbated by a storm and a lot of torrential rain. There were several storms during the month of August, 1995, but it was Tropical Storm Iris that severely overflooded and inflicted some damage to the foundation works.

The force of the water coming down from the hillside into the culvert below the main Morne Road, just east of my property, would overflow regularly, inflicting severe damage to the ongoing works which necessitated my seeking the intervention of the then Ministry of Communication and works, under its indefatigable and congenial minister, Gregory Avril, who facilitated truckloads of backfill material worth tens of thousands of dollars, which helped to ameliorate the costly effect of the devastation.

This development pleased my bankers who were obviously concerned about the mortgage which I had acquired from them. So they advised me to commission a photo shoot of the damage for insurance purposes. In a nutshell, everything came to a halt for several months to facilitate mopping up exercises and then to review the status of the works before charting the way forward. However, even with the ministry's intervention, I still had to seek an additional loan worth tens of thousands of dollars to complete the domestic and production studio complex.

In the interim there were also tremendous losses of building supplies; blocks, aggregate, sand, cement, steel, etc, due to the heavy rains, as well as significant levels of pilferage. So it is fair to say that I have never recovered from the destruction and the losses that had occurred. Sadly, it became the classic 'cost overruns' story that was far beyond my control.

Back Pains

One Sunday in early January 1996, I invited a couple to accompany me to a house warming at the home of Michael DuBoulay – a former Soufriere Member of Parliament who had just built a plantation house in the middle of his sprawling estate. We stopped at the Humming Bird Restaurant for drinks and when we were about ready to leave, I tried getting up and realized that I had some difficulty walking. I was in acute pain which got progressively worse. We still made it to the function though, at which the whole of Saint Lucia seemed to have been in attendance. I sat down most of the time as standing up proved to be unbearable. We left for Castries a lot sooner due to my condition and my friends literally had to lift me up from the vehicle to my CDC apartment. I tried to see a doctor that night with little success. The following day, I sought some medical attention at Victoria Hospital. I was examined and put on a rigid exercise programme for my lower back and legs, due to what was diagnosed as a pinched nerve in my lower back. I don't need to express my horror and fear at the prospect of being immobilized at still a youthful stage in my life. Fr. Q. learned of my situation and recommended that I see Mrs. Khan, a native Guyanese therapist, residing in Saint Lucia, who had a facility on Chaussee Road. He suggested that I was guaranteed relief if I went to see her. I did so and over a period of a year was able to walk reasonably well again, but with some discomfort at times. Mrs. Khan nursed me back to full health, not just because of her healing therapeutic hands but as a result of her constant prayers during those sessions.

Bats

During the summer of 1998, there was an incident with bats in my main bathroom. I do not know how the bats gained access to the bathtub, but thought I may have left one of the windows partially open which might have allowed the bats to come in. Hence I ensured that the windows remained shut whenever I demitted the house. One weekend, a close friend Alexis, was spending some time with me and after an evening out, I went into the bathroom and saw four bats in the bathtub. My mind was racing. I was beginning to think that maybe I was going crazy. So I called out to

Alexis and asked him what did he see in the bathtub and he confirmed that they were bats. He looked at me and asked where could they have come from since the windows were shut. I responded that I did not know. After a brief discussion on the matter, Alexis went to sleep.

A few minutes later I called out to the watchman seated on the porch downstairs, which was quite visible from my bedroom verandah. He had been listening to his radio. I asked him to come up to the room so that I could show him something. After first sourcing a black plastic bag in the kitchen downstairs, I showed him the bats in the bathtub and watched as he lifted each of the 4 bats and placed them into the bag. The last one he literally fondled on its nose, as one would have done to a cat or dog. I stood there in disbelief by what was taking place before me. Bats are despicable looking creatures and here was this man petting one of them. That stunned me! As he made his way downstairs I requested that he eradicated all of them immediately and remained watching every movement he made from a hidden vantage point, ensuring that I could not be seen. After sitting, he placed the partially opened bag in front of him, and allowed the bats to go off into the darkness. Shortly after, I noticed that the bats he had released seemed to have returned and were actually flying around him while he remained seated on the chair. I wanted to mention all of what I'd witnessed to Alexis but by then he was soundly asleep. So you could well imagine his disbelief when I recounted the late night experience to him the following day.

Christmas 1998 was the leanest advertising season ever for DSP and I had this sense that the clock was ticking away at our decade old existence. What a huge difference from former years when it was a challenge trying to please some two dozen plus clients who all wanted their Christmas television commercials very early; an impossibility of course!

It had become a tradition for my camera crew to vacation immediately after the Christmas bustle and they didn't return until mid-January, but Avril, my newly appointed Secretary, was back at work right after the holidays. It was one of those early January mornings when I discovered that my car had been broken into, the front window smashed and my Sony stereo system stolen. So it was under some stress that I informed the watchman about the incident. Not surprisingly he wasn't of any help, so that later, when Dunstan Fontenelle invited me to accompany him and a group to neighboring St. Vincent to participate in a Catholic Spiritual Retreat for a week, it just seemed a most welcome response to get away from Saint Lucia for a few days.

There were several participants form the neighboring islands and a couple of well known religious leaders from the US and the region as well. One of those persons that I met was Fr. Toss, a Saint Lucian Priest, resident in one of the parishes of St. Vincent. In one of the spiritual exercises, I told him about some of the bizarre experiences that I had encountered and after having listened patiently to me offered a 'Spiritual Warfare' prayer, which he had me to repeat after him, sentence after sentence. He said that I should make it a habit of saying that prayer on a daily basis which I did throughout the week. We met for a half hour just prior to my departure" "Dave!", He whispered, "your eyes have been closed, but I've prayed intensely for you during the week and on your return home, the scales will fall from your eyes and you will see and understand things that you've never seen or understood before. I saw an image of hands while I prayed over you" he said. "Hands?" I responded, mesmerized by his riveting account. "Yes!" Fr. Toss replied, "you will be fine."

I arrived home from St. Vincent at about 9:00 p.m., it was a Sunday and was surprised that the watchman was nowhere in sight. After parking and taking my travel bag indoors, I went down to his room via the kitchen and discovered that he had left the key in the lock, making it easy for anyone to gain access. The room was in complete darkness. So I turned on the light and found him soundly asleep. I woke him up and chided him for going to sleep at such an early hour, moreso with me off island and for not doing the job that he was being paid for. He mumbled some words that were incoherent, so I walked away leaving him in his stupor, all the while trying to internalize and cope with the deep sense of disappointment I felt.

In the coming days and weeks, I began to really see things around me that I'd never noticed before, as well as some of those in my immediate circle in a brand new way. It was almost as though I knew what they were thinking and about their modus operandi. In essence, I was seeing Saint Lucia, its people and everything in general through 'new eyes.'

Here are some of the bizarre experiences encountered.

January 1999 - Grapefruits

The secretary informed me that she had noticed two grapefruits that had been lying on the western doorsteps to my video production studio, and some 5 months later were still there, despite being exposed to the elements appearing as "fresh" as ever. I too had noticed the fruits and wondered about their origin. She said that she didn't have the presence of mind to inform me of this until then. We were at a loss as to who had placed them there, so I spoke to the watchman about it. He seemed somewhat cagey and upset when I asked him to remove them, which he did, and I insisted that they were both burnt, which occurred with the assistance of Mr. Cypal, a carpenter friend who was at the time working on a project for me.

February 1999 - Broken Cross Formation

I was heading to the bank one afternoon with Nick my accountant when he brought to my attention, several stones with leaves and grass amongst them, which was in the shape of a cross or half cross. I had never seen anything like it before even though they were just a few metres outside the entrance to the business section of the building. After having video taped the somewhat strange looking items, I drove to the church and met with Fr. St. Rose who recommended that I get some holy water in the church and purchase some salt which he would bless. He advised me to sprinkle some Holy Water and blessed salt on the strange looking formation. I remember explaining all this to Fr. Toss, whom I made contact with in St. Vincent the following day and he asked me to describe what I had witnessed, after which he dramatically announced that, "This was supposedly your grave," and that I should immediately dismiss the watchman whom I had permitted to reside in a small room in the basement. I had hired him on the advice of the building foreman sometime before the move to the new site in 1997, since at that time the building was somewhat vulnerable to burglary. Somewhat reluctantly, he dismantled the gravelike formation at my request. The following day Fr. St. Rose visited me to pray about all what was taking place. I dismissed the watchman a couple of days later. *In retrospect, I recall seeing the watchman always playing with stones at the office entrance and kept wondering what was the rationale for an elderly man playing with stones every time I entered the building particularly on evenings? It just seemed so weird.*

A few days later and in the presence of my accountant, I brought the watchman his pay cheque. He offered me his hand in a show of "no hard feelings!" but I had this sense that I shouldn't accept his handshake. He then lunged at me in a somewhat threatening manner, visibly upset that I hadn't accepted his peace sign. Fortunately, my Accountant Nick promptly came in between us so as to avoid any form of physical contact.

An hour or so later, under our watchful eyes, he was seen packing his few belongings which were transferred to a waiting pick-up truck just above the living quarters. Words cannot adequately describe the 'foul stench' that came out of the vacated room. It took us days to scrub, hose down, and use all sorts of disinfectants and deodorizers to clean the room. Additionally, with the help of a priest, we prayed and had holy water and blessed salt sprinkled both in, around and approaching the small room. I learnt a year or so later that he lived at Ciceron and was incapacitated for a few years until his death due to diabetes as he had lost both of his legs.

March 1999 - Locusts

One afternoon while in the office section of the building, my accountant caught a big brown locust trying to enter the window behind his desk, and because I was out, he placed it in an envelope for me to see. Days later, I found another brown locust on the master bedroom floor upstairs, but it was already dead. A couple of weekends later, while in the bathroom upstairs, (same area where the bats were discovered,) I noticed a strange looking insect on the bathroom wall. It was black with silver wings and had what appeared to be a crown on its head. I promptly went in search of a can of insecticide and, after having sprayed it for a few seconds, it fell to the floor and amazingly emitted what appeared to be blood. I was so taken aback by this, that I promptly shut the bathroom door and didn't return there until Nick showed up to work on Monday morning. On opening the bathroom door, his initial reaction was whether I had cut myself and when I told him that it had been the locust that had bled, he was as confused as I was. We then scooped it up. By then there was a foul stench, so we placed it in a plastic bag and burnt it, like we did the two others before.

April 1999 - Haitian Paintings

There was this large brightly coloured painting conspicuously located on one of the walls in the living room, as well as a smaller version of it opposite. One Sunday, Pastor Ben paid an unexpected call to my home. Because of some problems with his vehicle he came down from the road above my house to use the phone. We had produced his weekly programmes for some time and so he was a regular visitor. After I led him to the office, I was speaking in the living room to the young man who had accompanied him; "Do you know what the painting is all about?" he asked. I had only been drawn by the bright colours but had never really paid any attention to it, even though it had been there for nearly two years. The painting depicted some sort of ritual. There was a calf with a circle around it and a number of Haitian natives, numbering about 15, who knelt with heads bowed before it and they were all holding candles. The surprise on my face seemed to have brought some relief to the young man. He simply said, "I can tell that you didn't know that this painting portrayed some sort of demonic activity, and there was I already thinking that you must be involved in some crap." By then Pastor Ben had returned from making his call and suggested that I take down that painting, along with the smaller version and burn them, which is what I did with the help of my accountant the following day.

Broken Arms Ornamental Statue

Ornamental Statues have been immensely popular and can be seen in several gardens and living rooms of many homes. They are made of clay, some concrete with arms extended with some space at the top where the potted plants are placed. I had purchased three of them from a friend. Initially I discovered that one of the extended arms was broken somewhat mysteriously, which I placed in the area where the plant should have been. It was Dunstan Fontenelle (now deceased), on a visit to my home with his wife during Lent in 1998, who enquired about the broken arm, to which I couldn't offer a logical response. Then a few months later, the other arm was broken and so both arms were now occupying the vacant space which should have housed the plant. It was Alexis, who had witnessed the bats in the bathroom upstairs, who said to me on one of his visits in April, 1999, "Dave, how did the arms of the statue get broken?" he asked. It was obvious that someone had deliberately broken the two arms and the few persons that I related this incident to all echoed the same chorus, "Bwá Kasé." It was truly another bizarre occurrence.

There were also incidents with frogs seen regularly at the business entrance, as well as a massive termite infestation which seemed to have created a trail, going down into the production studio from a flamboyant tree in the grounds above. Tens of thousands of them, nested in the metal trunking of a Cable and Wireless telephone box that was conspicuous to staff and clients who walked through the office daily. It really was a shocking discovery. I also found a minature sized effigy made out of toilet paper that had been placed in a small hole behind a drywall partition just a few yards away from one of the two production studios. All sorts of things were going wrong: camera damage, computer and regular editing suite malfunctions, busted water pipes, smoke emitting from an electrical outlet, air condition dysfunction, strange and sudden vehicle malfunctions and all sorts of other unusual happenings.

Hidden Storeroom Items

One morning I was inspired to go to a storeroom downstairs, directly beneath my office and I discovered on a ledge to the right of the open door the following:

- A ruler standing vertically with a blue mark highlighting one of the numbers (can't remember now)

- A staple remover
- A big nail
- A small fuse (type used for electronic equipment and
- A small packet of black pepper with one end partially opened... some of the pepper had already seeped onto the ledge.

It's the consensus of persons extremely knowledgeable in such matters that all of the items highlighted represent something;

- The Ruler: Indicates a time frame of some months or possibly years.
- Staple Remover: An important secretarial tool.
- Nail: Symbolic of carpentry works that were on going around the property.
- Fuse: Without which some important audio/video equipment would cease to function.
- Black Pepper: Denotes provocation, divisive and quarrelsome environment.

So its any body's guess why these items were positioned in the manner that they were, hidden away from my eyesight. In essence it was very much a chance discovery but it does make you wonder how and why these items were placed there and for how long before being discovered.

May 1999 - More Stress

Several years ago, a certain group of persons was indebted to me in the sum of several thousand dollars. All attempts to recover the finance proved futile. Then one day at my wits end, I contacted Fr. Toss, who was in neighbouring St. Vincent and after his suggestions of prayer and fasting, I made a startling discovery: 'the letters of the peoples names, when put together confirmed their participation in 'demonic worship activity'. I don't have to mention how shocked Fr. Toss and the other priests whom I had confided in were. Hence it was all that and the other bizarre developments which prompted me to go on a pilgrimage to Betania in Venezuela that

December, the very eve of the new millennium and the truly miraculous events witnessed during that trip.

Home Masses

By then Fr. Goodman had blessed both the interior and exterior of the building and held two masses in the very living room where occultic activity had taken place, and the building was also consecrated to the Sacred Heart of Jesus and the Immaculate Heart of Mary.

I recall just prior to the first mass being said that Fr. Goodman didn't show up at the scheduled time. So fearing the worst I called him at the Jacmel Presbytery, where he confirmed that he had suddenly felt ill about an hour or so before his visit, but assured me that I need not worry as he was going to keep his commitment regardless, much to the joy of the small group of us who awaited him in the living room of my home. The second Mass was held a month later. On both occasions some incredible things occurred to me on the days following the Masses which really confirmed what I'd always heard from the Catholic Church that "the Mass is the most efficacious and powerful prayer". Three other Masses were said during the first six months of the year 2000.

June 1999 - Accounts Receivables

During that period (January-August) we had a lot of difficulty in the collection of the company's receivables, some as old as 6 months. However, I soon came to the realization right after the locust incident, that several businesses called to inform us that long outstanding cheques were suddenly available for collection. It was truly a welcome development.

I took my licks. The rumor mill too was awash with all kinds of claims, some of which I believe were being spread by my competitors. It was as though all the negative forces out there had come together to fight us. It was unbearable. I believe too that it was because of my faith in God that I retained my sanity much to the surprise of my detractors, some of whom had already predicted my doom. Fr. Goodman, Fr. Toss and Fr. St. Rose helped me immensely. I went through a spiritual renaissance; I prayed a lot, went to regular confession and to daily Mass, received the Holy Eucharist often, prayed before the Blessed Sacrament, said the Holy Rosary and the Chaplet of Divine Mercy daily. My newly- found spirituality gave me the inner strength needed to overcome all the daily challenges and so even when some of my friends and acquaintances deserted me, I was able to overcome the hurt and disappointment. If anything, it made me stronger. The period 1999-2002 was extremely rough but looking back, its made me all the more resilient today.

Visions:

My accountant told me of several visions that he had. Here are a few that have left an indelible print in my mind.

- That he was coming down the incline to my house and he noticed that I was talking to a lady on the patio above my office. The lady's back was towards him so he couldn't see her face and he thought he heard me use the word "Construction" in my discussion with her. A bit later he says, he felt hungry and ventured into my office and discovered that I had 5 loaves in a bag and decided to eat one. He returned a few moments later to have another loaf and it was then he heard some voices and some laughter in the adjoining room. (living room) He therefore opened the door ever so slightly and witnessed that my living room had been transformed into a tabernacle with white painted walls and green drapery. He would also accompany me to a couple of cenacles at Mount Calvary where I prayed with a men's group every Wednesday afternoon, and was also present at the first two masses by Fr. Goodman in the living room of my house.

- Another time there was a party in the living room with music, laughter and merriment. For some reason my accountant says that he was compelled to go downstairs away from the activity. There he discovered a bag which contained a lot of jewelry and precious stones. He says that he was tempted to keep some of the precious gems for himself, but an inner voice within told him to bring it to the attention of the home owner.

Mystery Caller?

The accountant also related to me an incident which had occurred when he received a call at his home but at the section in which his mom resided. This was very unusual as calls came to him directly downstairs where he lived with his wife. He explains "on picking up the receiver, there was a lot of static and a voice which seemed to be from "Another Realm" was making enquires about the author. Could he confirm that I was a prayerful individual and a regular church goer?" which he confirmed and then shortly after, the caller hung up.

Then secondly, he said that he had a vision of an angelic form that could be seen flying over the city and hordes of people below were looking up and pointing. It amazes me how God would use an employee to relate those visions to me.

Da Mister

1999 is drawing to a close. It's late morning and my secretary informs me that there's a call from da mister. I picked up the phone and heard nothing for a while. When I answered 'Hello!', a female voice told me to hold on for da mister who engaged me in some small talk. How were things? Challenges in the past year and hopes for the new year 2000 and wished me A Happy New Year! The caller finally blurted. "Oh I hear you're always in Church so I guess that's not a bad thing right?" I merely laughed and wished da mister the best for the New Year as well.

Fast Forward

A few weeks after returning from a Pilgrimage in Betania, and at the start of the new year 2000, I was at the Morning mass at St. Benedict's church, just down the road from my home. I felt my nose about to drip just after the consecration of the host so I went outside to blow my nose. It was all very odd because I didn't have a cold. I blew a lot of stuff; brown, yellow and green mucus into a paper towel and returned to the mass shortly after. It truly was an extraordinary moment and I've often wondered, "what was that all about?"

In the elections of 2001, I got some work from the UWP and was able to generate some income. I think some of my rivals retaliated against me because I had produced material for that organisation under Dr. Morella Joseph. I think that was the price I paid. By then my company DSP had already folded up, leaving me with a mountain of debt but with my sanity intact.

The following statement is from Fr. Lambert St. Rose, whose intervention I sought during my JOB Experience. It is to his credit and other priests, through the grace of GOD that I'm alive today. Fr. St. Rose has rescued many from the clutches of the evil one and his minions by his many exorcisms, throughout the length and breath of our nation.

You would do well to get some more insight from his **book "In Turbulent Waters"**.

STATEMENT:

In a world grown cold, insensitive, disengaged and callously individualistic, ravenously secularized, materialistic and naively nihilistic in its outlook of life and personal achievements; where its inhabitants are incredibly and rapidly becoming isolationists and the robotical culture is alarmingly becoming more and more entrenched through the courtesies of modern technology; where all the above have supplanted authentic religion, and left in their wake, a thin veneer of religiousity as a mask of pretense, it is no surprise that Satan is on a rampage, and what he did not achieve through his assaults on Job and on Jesus, have been gullibly embraced by those who claim to be atheists, agnostics and purport a form of pelagianism in support of the laxism which assists them in proffering their unconscionable callousness without scruples.

Given this historical nightmarish social, political, economic cum religious and human conditions which have now engulfed the world, the hearts of men, women and children alike, it should be no surprise to us, to find there are still many Jobs lingering in ash pits, inflicted by invisible and mysterious scabs searching the heavens for an answer and solution and a way out of their nightmare which sometime seems overtly and willfully delayed despite their innocence.

Dave Samuels is one of the many victims who have wandered into my path seeking help out of his hellish conditions. I know and believe there is a God and a heaven; I also know Satan and hell exist. Just as I know there are fervent Christians; I also know there are devout Satanists – living, walking and working in disguise in full view of all of us: they are bent on destroying, obstructing and depriving others of achieving their full potential for their myopic gains, thinking it is for the aggrandizement – but, literally, they are fools who will subsequently be brought to naught, at the appointed time. For good always triumphs over evil.

Dave was for a time "A Job-man" living in our midst, physically. He looked healthy at the time, but his life was a living hell, and his tormentors and competitors exploited every opportunity within the structures of his business to wipe him out of the business landscape. Fetishism was not part of Dave's belief, but when suspicious objects, bloody smears, flashing shadows, unusual stenches, sound of heavy trampling footsteps followed by frequent destruction of his tools of trade, he had a rude awakening that something was amiss.

At that time Dave's faith, although not too strong, yet contrary to what many of his typical country folk would do, he did not turn to the traditional *gadè* (witch doctor) for help. Like Job, he turned to his God, his faith increased and through the help of his spiritual guides, one day like Job, Dave was born again.

J. Lambert St. Rose

CHAPTER 6

"CLICK" RSL 97

*"One serious malaise of our society today is the seeming inability
of too many people to keep their word or promise on a simple
agreement." (Willie James – Broadcaster and Journalist)*

The new millennium had begun to unleash a proliferation of radio stations
across Saint Lucia. The broadcasting technology had changed and it was
now easy for any one-man outfit to broadcast, radio as we knew it in the
past four decades had died. But with the change came a corresponding
drop in quality and standards. Saint Lucians were now being fed almost
anything in the name of radio and the new generation that had never
known better was accepting it.

In Willie James' book "St. Lucia Land of Intriguing Romances" he writes
about the French priests-teachers initiative in the rural areas, out of
which emerged distortions of mispronunciation now endemic in the Saint
Lucian English expression. Even today James opines "University graduates
teaching in our schools, fail to pronounce properly words such as category,
committee, study and a litany of others. The French priests-teachers were
perhaps not the very best teachers of English. The intention was noble, well
meaning and they gave of their best and that best was a cultural tragedy
and what we are and where we are" What Willie James has highlighted is
prevalent from some announcers on several radio stations in Saint Lucia,
which is an affront to best broadcasting practice. Here are some examples:

SIX is pronounced SEEKS; SHIP is SHEEP and SHEEP is SHIP; IS is EASE and WIN is WEAN, while WIND is WEEN; SPIN is SPEEN; HILL is HEEL; while HEEL is HILL; WITH is WIFF or WEEF; STUDY is STURDY; WILL is WHEEL; THIRTEEN is FAIRTEEN; IT is EAT; PUSH IT is POOSSH EAT; PASSENGERS is PA-SIN-GERS; LIVE is LEAVE and LEAVE is LIVE; FULL is FOOL; PULL IT is POOL EAT; MISS is MEESE; DIG is DEEG; Just a few examples of the aberration of English by the French influence.

However, there is still a very sizeable section of the population that grew up on good radio and wanted to listen to well spoken announcers, presenting programs of quality and substance.

In 2002, right after the General Elections, Jeff Fedee took over as Chairman of RSL and that's how I went back there. RSL had by then deteriorated and he was looking for a few people to enhance programming so I did some freelancing and introduced the program "Coffee Break at Sandals."

The guests would come in to discuss the issues of the day: political, social, and just about everything, and at the end would have breakfast with me compliments of the hotel. The program went on for about four years. Among my guests were Governor General Dame Pearlette Louisy, Prime Minister Kenny Anthony, Sir John Compton, Sir Dunstan St. Omer, Charles Cadet, Lady Gladys Lewis, wife of Sir Arthur, Publisher Rick Wayne, community, social, religious and political leaders. We also did interviews with several artistes and had them to perform live from the area especially around the Christmas, Jazz and Carnival Seasons. For a while, I tried to expand the show, but management felt that there were already too many talk shows around, an argument which to me was debatable.

I've always suspected, but to be fair cannot verify with certainty, occasions when Coffee Break at Sandals couldn't be broadcast, because of so called technical glitches, and I'm not suggesting that there wouldn't be times when this will occur but "I came away with the impression that the powers that be, didn't want certain persons to be heard on the air," so the program may have been sabotaged. There were even some subtle attempts to neutralize and even silence me, especially when I was on air with some UWP Operatives. Some people act that because they were in charge, they could do anything to you; shaft you, lie about you, demerit you, and look through you as though you didn't exist.

There was a period in which I felt so detached that I discontinued watching and listening to local news and reading the local newspapers and even stopped attending cultural and sporting events. I felt so disconnected from everyone and everything that was taking place around me, even friends and family who had been constant visitors and callers too, all seemed to have deserted me, except for a handful. I often heard echoes of Granny's advice to me when I was growing up, *"Pa worry ich moi, yo pa Bondye,"* (Don't worry my child, they're not God.) It was a balm towards my drooping spirit, and which brought consolation to my heart.

At RSL, I always felt that there were some staffers who liked things to remain as they were and didn't want to see the station progress. Many were intimidated at being "Shown up" and besides, it was a sort of haven for people of a particular mind set, who were there to do the bidding of the political directorate even when it was 'De Classe', and every guest who was linked to the other party, or who just had a different political viewpoint was the source of derision in the newsroom. I was amazed by the number of guests who would comment on the attitudes they encountered just before and after the show as they walked through the newsroom. It was sad at what RSL had become, staffed by a small bunch who were in the main indifferent and unproductive, but being encouraged and rewarded for their negative attitudes and that was fine, because they supported *"De Partee"*, rather than use their status to edify and unify the people of Saint Lucia.

I'd like to give a snap shot of some of my personal experiences. On one of my Saturday Morning programs, I recall making some comments about the desirability for good on air announcers, as most of the current crop just viewed the profession as a popularity contest, rather than an opportunity to shape and mold the minds of the listener. 'Announcers from all radio stations must share the blame and work on producing material to impact and enhance people's lives, and that even RSL was not exempt'. I don't have to tell you the extent to which I was excoriated. A few days later I was summoned to a Heads of Department meeting and sadly, the interest was not so much in what was articulated, but rather, whom was I referring to.

Then there was the issue of covering live events i.e: Carnival, Jazz, etc, and because of the religiosity of some people, there was usually an unexplained cut off broadcast point, (three or more hours before the scheduled close) because of their church event the following day, so that the general listenership was deprived of the outcome of the LIVE proceedings, undermining the purpose of the broadcast in the first place. It was obvious that some members of that click put their religion before their jobs. Many times I confronted very strong anti-Catholic, anti big religion biases, particularly when I interviewed those guests who didn't belong to their faith. Also, some young and budding announcers left the job due to lack of guidance and direction, as promises made to them were broken and their eagerness to produce creative programs stifled, simply because the head of programs showed no interest in their vision.

There was also the unfortunate treatment meted out to the Grenadian born, Saint Lucian based veteran broadcaster Vaughn Noel, aka The Bumble Bee, whom I grew up listening to, arguably the most recognized voice on radio. He was a gem of a human being who was deliberately exploited because of his love for radio. He never said "No!" whenever requested to fill in for anyone, usually at very short notice. There were times he worked from 5:00 a.m to 3:00 p.m or from 2:00 pm- Midnight: 10 long hours, because his relief announcer was unable to show up for various reasons and recognizing that I lived a short distance away, he would call me to request something to eat, which I was always happy to provide. I pray God forgives all those who used and maltreated the Bumble in every way possible. May he rest in peace.

One afternoon, while walking towards my car from the station, I crossed paths with this Department Head, and he said something to the extent that "RSL was too much of a small place for the two of us". Just like that! I sat down in my car for at least 5 minutes afterwards, trying to decipher what would prompt any human being to make such an incredulous and unconscionable statement like that, when they had no means of determining whether they were going to survive the next day, far less the next few hours.

I had just concluded an interview with MP for Castries South East, Menissa Rambally, during which I used voice clips from Guy Mayers, at the time the head of the Saint Lucia Chamber of Commerce, who cited certain concerns which he had with the Government through her, and she did a wonderful job at responding to these concerns. Lo and behold on returning to our Morne Studios, the General Manager, Roger Joseph (R.J.) quipped "Oh, that Mayers insert was about seven minutes, which was much too long," so I replied "Wrong Sir" the insert was a little less than 2 ½ minutes". He rebutted, "well it sounded like seven minutes to me" and walked away without so much as an apology.

In 2003, I recorded an interview with George Odlum a few weeks before he died, but decided to use at a later stage, and since the fourth anniversary of his death was approaching in 2007, promoted the interview that I would have presented along with family members Jon and Buffalo Odlum, who would have been live on Coffee Break with me. However, one day before, the GM requested the tape. He proceeded to edit the interview from a half hour to about 14 minutes, without even seeking my participation or views on the matter.

In the interview Odlum expounded on his reasons for leaving the Kenny D. Anthony Administration (KDA) and felt that he was being undermined and neutralized by party members. The genesis of the story goes like this, that he Odlum, sometime around late 1997 early 1998 had obtained the support of most of his cabinet colleagues in pursuing at the time, diplomatic relations with mainland China rather than Taiwan. It appeared that KDA preferred Taiwan at the time and Odlum suggested that since that issue he was a marked man. In other words, "if a sitting Prime Minister does not have a consensus vote by his cabinet colleagues on such an important matter, then it was clear the discomfort he would feel moving forward on any other matter of national importance, even that of his own tenure as Prime Minister?" Of course up to this day I have not been able to confirm that story, but there are many people who say that this was in fact the case.

After many months I eventually received confirmation from Sandals Resorts International, that Chairman and Owner Butch Stewart had agreed to be a guest on Coffee Break. My enthusiasm was cut short however, when the technician told me that it wasn't going to be possible to broadcast from the Sandals Grande because of some challenges. There was simply "no interest, no accommodating tone, or, I'll look into it." Simply, "Its not possible!" but for the intervention of the new Managing Director, it eventually worked out.

So that is what I experienced at RSL from 2003 – 2008; a far cry from the incredibly wonderful salad days of the 1970s, when we would have discussions and arguments on many important matters. Of course there was always room for banter and jocular debates, but there's a general tendency in today's media and just about every watering hole, to "put people down" "hurl insults, criticize, peddle rumour, make up stories without the facts-Fake News perhaps? Most of the conversation was and still is 90% politically driven. It seems almost an excuse to avoid serious discourse on the many social and economic challenges that confront us.

There were four highlights of my stint though. The presentation of Wake Up Saturday, created a great deal of hype in the morning, targeting those heading to work and to market, engaged in household chores or who just loved listening to up tempo Caribbean and local music; Calypso, Soca, Zouk, Compa from 6:00 -10:00 a.m every Saturday hosted by yours truly for about 5 years.

Then on Sundays, "Golden Memories" from 3:00 -7:00 p.m, playing all the Oldie Goldies from the late 50s, 60s, through to the 90s. It was definitely my favorite, playing music with a particular target audience in mind. Music seldom heard on the airwaves these days.

Ella, Satchmo, Nat King Cole, Perry Como, Sarah Vaughan, Billy Holiday, Dionne Warwick, Nancy Wilson, Aretha Franklin, Dinah Washington, Ann Murray, Frank Sinatra, Sammy Davis, Dean Martin, Elvis Presley, The Platters, The Beatles, The B-Gees, The Letterman, Tony Bennett, Barbara Streisand, Roger Whittaker, Natalie Cole, Diana Ross, The

Supremes, The Temptations, The Stylistics, Marvin Gaye, Sam Cook, John Denver, Elton John, Stevie Wonder, Luther Vandross, Lou Rawls, Air Supply, Brook Benton, Percy Sledge, Ottis Redding, Michael Jackson etc. etc. plus some of the big bands and great orchestras of my generation. Need I go on? How often do you hear such great music on any of our radio stations today? Nuff said! I know I must have made a number of you nostalgic and it feels good just doing that huh?

There was also the memorable staging of the "Sparrow Gold Show in December 2005, at the Pigeon Island National Landmark at which over 3000 people turned out to. It was the Birdie at his scintillating best along with his band, belting out number after number and the absolutely sizzling party atmosphere at the end. That's how we'd all like to remember The Sparrow. There were also appearances by many of our local calypso monarchs.

Then the live broadcast which some of us anchored from the Minor Basilica of the Immaculate Conception -the State Funeral of Prime Minister Sir John, on September 18, 2007. It was a very sad and somber day in our country's history, but a great opportunity to give the world the biography of the man, and with Saint Lucians in the Diaspora and the international media linking with us, we were able to provide some excellent commentaries, and R.J. deserves commendations for his support of those two phenomenal events in particular.

After the departure of R.J., Ms. Mary Polius succeeded him as Managing Director and reflects on the initial period of her stint. "The multiplicity of challenges that plagued Radio Saint Lucia was discovered very early on the job, a decrepit building in dire need of renovation, the receivables were large and for the most part over 6 years old and uncollectable. There were outstanding payables to key organizations including NIC and ECCO. The staff were untrained and unmotivated and the station received a paltry subvention from the Government, but it was not all doom and gloom as my predecessor had done a phenomenal job with the structure of the organization, which I understand was non-existent before his time. However, for the compilation of short, medium and long term goals, a true appreciation of the status of the station's finances, program and staff capacity was required, and therefore reviews and audits were conducted. Radio Saint Lucia, unlike some stations did not own a day-time talk program. When the idea of introducing such a program was introduced, some middle managers were quite vociferous against it, citing that it would simply be more of the same and would not generate revenue for the station. The opposition was palpable, but posed no deterrent", recalls Ms. Polius.

That's how "The Agenda" began. I developed a strict code of conduct for public participation: callers to the program were to treat my guests with courtesy and respect and refrain from boisterous or offensive language. Personally, I felt there was the need to uplift the standard of discussion over the media generally. There was just too much bitterness being displayed, too much negativity, too much sniping here and there, gossiping and character assassination and the regular overdose of political partisanship that had made so many turn off talk programs. Instead, we committed to mirror positivity as much as possible, encouraging callers to submit ideas and solutions to the myriad problems facing the country and its people. So the mandate was to edify, educate and entertain, to give everyone a chance to express themselves on the specific topics being discussed even when I, as host, disagreed with their views. Additionally, we did not subscribe to seeking confrontation with our guests or hurling insults at callers as we believed that all views should be allowed to contend.

So its back to Ms Polius. "Upon presentation of the idea to the Board of Directors, it was fully embraced, and they gave their blessings. Less than two months later, The Agenda, as the program was dubbed, took to the airwaves with host David Samuels, well known media personality who was no stranger to the then *RSL-The Sun Station*. A small scale rebranding exercise followed and gave birth to RSL 97 and a new tagline, "*The Experience*". Within record time The Agenda became the most popular and lucrative program on RSL 97 and almost totally eclipsed the News Nationwide at 1:00 pm. During my four year tenure at RSL 97, The Agenda raked in an average of $25K monthly and contrary to the skepticism expressed, became a household name and hosted an extensive cadre of guests and discussed diverse issues and topics of national interests.

The Agenda also earned its place on the talk show landscape as being balanced, unbiased and apolitical. The Opposition was given the same opportunity as the incumbent and it was gratifying to note the frequency with which they accepted invitations to be on the program. There were challenges sometimes as the station pressed on to fulfill its mandate, and I recall the difficulties we encountered in getting Government technocrats to be available to disseminate information to the citizenry. Being the Nation's station with a mandate such as we had, information sharing especially from Government departments should have been an integral part of our programming but it was not so. In fact, sourcing guests from the private sector was simpler and required far less effort. There was an instance when for months ahead of Budget Presentation, we tried to get a government employee or two to speak to the preparation of the Budget but it never happened."

Continued the former Managing Director – "Through the sheer credibility of the program and the host, advertisers were prepared to pay to be guests on *The Agenda*. And that too, became another revenue stream for the program. The rising popularity of the program was no accident as behind the scenes there were people contributing to sourcing material and involved in its production. There were routine reviews to ensure that there was no deviation from the intent and objective, which was to provide information for empowerment. The many years of experience of the host, who had become known as Mr. Chairman was the catalyst for the success of *The Agenda*. The shows ranged from being titillating to ultra serious issues, yet all with powerful lessons for the edification of the audience". Ms Polius concluded. "The commendations were numerous, the accolades came pouring in and then all of a sudden the program was yanked off the air 'until further notice'. A new administration had been installed by the people, and their first order of business was to dismantle a program that had served the people well, simply in the name of petty politics! Revenue for the station plummeted".

Sometime around mid-January, 2012, I received a call from Ms Polius, confirming that she had just got a letter from the Ministry of Information and Broadcasting saying that all talk shows and programs had to be discontinued immediately, until the new Board determined which direction they wanted the station to go. I knew right away that "The days of the Agenda" were over.

I picked up my last cheque in October 2012, but what was most heart wrenching was that there was not one comment from anyone, no official letter of explanation, nothing from the Board, nothing from the management, Nothing! So ended another chapter in my life.

RSL97 was officially shut down on July 31, 2017, and its staff sent home. Reports indicate that termination benefits were amicably negotiated on behalf of the employees by its union, the Civil Service Association (CSA) the bargaining agents for over 40 years.

That there was some uproar when 90 minutes was taken off the air defies any logic, especially by some people whom I respect for their contribution to media. The host was openly and publicly associated with the former administration and should have done the honorable thing with the advent of a new administration, resign and move on, but he chose to remain, bashing the new administration as though they were still in opposition and appeared to be orchestrating and encouraging pro opposition surrogates and callers, in their castigation of the barely 4 month old Government and to rub some salt to the wound, proclaimed that his contract had been extended for a couple more years by his former bosses, on the eve of the June 6, 2016, General Elections. All of these were extraordinary, bizarre, highly irregular and contentious moments, so it came as no surprise when the program was eventually taken off the air.

I do not wish to take sides as to whether the station should have been closed or not, because I'm conflicted on the matter. As an RSL boy, I am completely aware of all the challenges: Uninspiring programs, under performing workers and some bad business practices which occurred there for many years. Administrations past must share some of the blame for utilizing the station to operate as a "Propaganda Network" at the expense of the Saint Lucian taxpayers, for employing people many of whom who lacked the requisite skills and generally known as operatives of de party in power. When most radio stations had 8-12 staffers, RSL had nearly 36 and at one point almost 50 people on its payroll. So it comes as no surprise that the station has been a financial disaster for the last 20 years at least. One may wish to argue that the closure seems draconian, but I will reserve judgment and observe how the Allen Chastanet Administration deals with this controversial matter, in the short to medium term.

I missed RSL tremendously during the passage of Hurricane Maria and would like to join many in a call for a national broadcast system. For several years Saint Lucian folk tuning to RSL could rely on credible information on impending weather systems from the Meteological and NEMO offices, essential services, related agencies, as well as from listeners who were always willing to share their personal experiences and the goings on in their community. It was always so reassuring to hear those voices and that of the announcers who worked tirelessly throughout the night, reassuring us that we were not alone, that we were all facing this potential weather threat together.

However during Maria, information was sketchy and came to us via our mobile phones, some radio and television stations, and we all know that the phones would probably be the first to be affected should the worst occur during a weather system. Then amazingly, we heard from the NEMO director that some of the information communicated to us on our mobiles was inaccurate and was most probably FAKE NEWS. Now! Isn't that cause for concern?

After the clearance was given, and when interacting with several people in the days following, I discovered that many appeared to be generally uninformed about the state of the country, the situation with schools, work, health and emergency services and the condition of the road network etc. We need to develop a radio system that citizens can rely on during a national emergency. What happened during the passage of Hurricane Maria exposed many flaws and weaknesses in the system, and that should not be occurring in 2017. We can and must do better!

CHAPTER 7

PASSAGES

"Your Father loved older women and I would secretly
observe him chatting them at every opportunity."
My Mom-2003..

If I have not had much to say about my dad, David Zachary Samuels, it is only because there is so little that I know about him. Originally from Antigua, he was connected in some way with the Colonial Development Corporation (CDC), the British group that built what are commonly known as the CDC Block apartments in Castries following the disastrous fire of 1948. He may have well been the reason why my family was able to secure one of the apartments. Three years after marrying my mother, he left Saint Lucia for the United Kingdom. She followed him there four years later and divorced him in 1962.

After the divorce, he married Silke, a German Native and had three girls and a son by her. I have been in touch with one of the girls. It appears that he was also something of a ladies' man, as he had a couple of other children in Antigua before marrying my mother in Saint Lucia. For a while I was also in touch with another sister in the U.S. who has since kept ties with his family, especially nieces and nephews in Tortola, St. Thomas, St. Croix and Antigua.

In April, 2013, I received an email from Jeanette Louis Brown (formerly Samuel) residing in Delaware, USA, who informed me that she was the first born of David Z. Samuels, and had attempted in years past to find out more about her father. She said that she was born in Gray's Hill, Antigua, on April 11, 1940, and her mother's name was Bernice, who had passed some 20 years ago and was heartbroken due to the whereabouts of David Z, with whom she had lost early contact with during his years in Saint Lucia and then later England. Jeanette said that her mother had told her once that David Z was unable to support them financially, as the seasonal change required him to wear appropriate clothing, which had impacted negatively on his disposable income. She also confirmed that she had a brother "Jerome" whom David Z had by another mother and who would have been 2 years younger than she was. "Jerome was in England for a few years while I was there studying in the late 50's, but lost contact with him when he was shipped out to the military and was stationed in Germany", Jeanette concluded. "Aunt Gwenyth, his sister, knew her well, but seemed reluctant to mention her father to her and that she was unaware of the additional (S) to their family name and wondered what the story about that was". I have also come to know another sister, Bettina, and through her, additional details of my father have come to light.

So how does a brother thousands of miles away get to know about his late father's children in, of all places, Germany? Well around that same period, I received a call from St. Thomas and the person introduced himself as Vincent Samuel. He enquired if my name was David Samuels and I confirmed that it was. He asked me if I had family in Antigua, if David Z was my father, if Gwenyth Perry was my aunt, and I replied to all his questions in the affirmative. He continued "I've been trying to make contact with you for many years. You see I am your nephew; I am the son of Winston. I've lived with Clyna, my grandmother, who conceived Winston for your father (my grandfather). Shortly after he was born, David Z suddenly left Antigua for Saint Lucia we were told and was never heard from again." You can well imagine how astounded I was to receive all this news in the space of a half hour or so.

Vincent Jahmore Samuel, Assistant Professor of Accounting and Finance, at the University of the Virgin Island in St. Thomas, would continue to keep in touch via phone calls and email and I got to learn a lot about my father's side of the family in Antigua and Tortola in particular, but there were other family members in St. Croix, St. Thomas and further afield. I also learnt that my brother, Winston, his father had passed away in 1998, after a long battle with diabetes.

It is to the credit of Vincent that I have learnt of my Antiguan paternal grand parents, Joseph and Rhonda Samuel, and that my dad had seven brothers and a sister, the latter whom I had already met in Antigua in the mid 90's and an uncle William Alexander Samuels, whose funeral I attended in Tortola in 1999, during which time I met several members of the Samuels clan, including an uncle Abraham from St. Croix, who passed a year later and my cousin Dag, an athletics coach, who tragically passed during the passage of Hurricane Irma in September, 2017. Also it is Vincent who never stopped searching for family and who was able to connect the dots with David Z and my German siblings.

It appears that David Z intended to study to become a doctor when he left Saint Lucia for England. He met and had an affair for a short while with a Swedish woman and they had a daughter, Jenny, but we do not know much more about this love story, except that Jenny and her mother returned to Sweden. Then about 1958 he met Silke, an assistant to a family in London. Silke's parents apparently operated a guest house business in Helgoland, Germany, but soon thereafter her father died and she was forced to return to Helgoland to support her mother with their guesthouses, but on several occasions she traveled back to London and, as life goes, she became pregnant. In November of 1960, she gave birth to a baby boy Dirk, but Silke and David Z didn't marry until June 1962.

Other children with Silke came. Nicolle was born in 1963. However, it was only after her birth in February, 1964, says Bettina, that David Z moved from London to Helgoland permanently. Jeanette was born the following year, 1965. "At this time my grandmother was alive and she accepted him and the marriage. This was very unusual for German people after the Second World War and David Z respected her. Bettina said that her siblings and herself were a bit uprooted not only from relatives, but from their culture, as they were not even used to meeting other black people in

Germany or to speak English regularly. "We learned to keep our distance. Additionally, each of us had to fight the negative effects of the inter-racial relationship between our parents. Meanwhile David Z integrated himself into the German Society and became extremely popular. Bettina remembers that when she was about eight or nine, Jenny, the Swede, visited her family in Helgoland to learn more about her father but they never saw her again.

Bettina also recalls that when she and the others were little, there was a wooden chest in their parents' bedroom. They often opened this trunk because on the inside there was a bag which always attracted their interest. This bag contained "a lot of different small tubes, small bottles and a range of medical instruments. We loved to play doctors' games secretly with it". According to Bettina, David Z passed himself off as a doctor in Helgoland, but he never had a permit to practice in Germany so that it wasn't possible for him to work in the medical profession. In fact, she remembered that her mother always doubted if he had ever completed his medical degree.

As far as the man himself was concerned, Bettina remembers him as being endowed with the gift of very good articulation and excellent manners. He was good looking and had his own special charm and it was easy to be captivated by his personality. David Z placed very great value on his external appearance, clothing himself, privately and publicly, with great elegance. He was always dressed in suits of top quality with vest and tie and when out, he wore a hat and business shoes. When it rained, he even covered his shoes with rubbers. In bed he wore silk pajamas and he also protected his hair with a night cap. At 1.90m. tall with his slim body, he looked very attractive. As someone who had come from the other side of the world, he was regarded as an interesting personality by many people and he sought to enhance his reputation by learning to speak German quickly. "At the same time we kids learned to talk, he started to learn the German language. Adults can learn a lot from children and it worked; he communicated with us solely in German, word by word. To educate us, on the other hand, in English, was never his interest", said Bettina.

Just recently I goggled information on Helgoland (also spelt Heligoland), and I discovered that it is a small German archipelago in the North Sea, consisting of two islands but only one is populated with an area of one sq mile (km) and the other is visited for its beautiful "beaches" during summer time. The islands are some 29 miles off the German coastline and were at one time Danish and then later British possessions. Helgoland boasts fabulous tourist resorts for the German upper class and remains a popular tourist destination for one day ship cruises, perhaps for its well known duty free status.

So it was there that David Z lived for over a decade, the only black person with his mixed race family in a population of just over a thousand Caucasian people. I can very well imagine the attention that this black man must have received wherever he went, more so as there was almost total absence of car traffic. He must have been the center of attraction indeed!

"The marriage with Silke was being undermined and challenged due to David Z's romantic escapades at some of the night clubs and other social meeting spots in Helgoland and Hamburg, creating irreconcilable differences between them, which led to a divorce about 1971, but he didn't move out of the family guest house complex until 1975 to live with his girlfriend Margaret in Hamburg, where contact was lost for some time, but our mother had informed us about the incurable illness which he had. We felt very sorry for him, but he was not playing any role in our lives anymore" recalls Bettina.

A few years later, my brother Dirk recalls the last encounter with David Z; "I met him in the summer of 1980 at the request of my mother, at the flat of his girlfriend Margaret in the downtown Hamburg area. I was 19 years old and my plan was to face and reproach him for all his shenanigans. I was angry at him. She opened the door and kindly led me to the living room where he was seated in an armchair. I immediately noticed how sick he was. He was too weak to stand up. My anger vanished almost instantly. We talked about superficialities, you know, nothing of much importance. It was really a short visit. Next thing I heard about him, was that he died in a hospital in November of that year" concluded Dirk. Bettina said that she does not know if he was remorseful before he died, but at his funeral, the song 'We shall overcome' was played, which she understood was his last wish, and that suggested to her, that he felt himself more than a victim. Silke remarried and passed on New Years' Day, 2013 and Margaret in 2014. David Z left behind the following children:

Jeanette and Jerome residing in the USA   Winston - Antigua (deceased)
David C. - Saint Lucia   Jenny, Sweden
Dirk, Nicolle, Jeanette, Bettina, Oliver - Germany

As I said earlier, much of my early years were spent under the guidance of my grandmother, Clerona. After my parents divorced my mother returned to Saint Lucia just briefly, but was gone again with "Smitty" to the Dutch island of Curacao. They had known each other for several years and had kept in touch before, during and after her divorce. He too was a divorcee. They got married in 1963. Smith was involved in sports, and a highly respected baseball coach in the Dutch Antilles. His passion for introducing little league is legendary in the Dutch Antilles, which has resulted in him being honored in the Hall of Fame. He eventually became an umpire who travelled all over Central America and Cuba officiating at matches. By this time she was a housewife while Ernie was also a salesman working for a very well established car dealership. Both of them came to Saint Lucia from time to time.

One day, in August, 1982, there was a loud knock on the door of my CDC apartment. I got up, opened the door and there standing outside was the tall, strapping, imposing figure of Ernest Smith, my stepfather. He said he was just returning from umpiring a series of matches in Central America and decided that, before returning to Curacao, he wanted to see family in Saint Lucia. We spent most of the day together which included a visit to Mon Repos to see his maternal and paternal relatives as well as his mother and sisters in Castries who were elated at the surprise visit. Smith had not been to Saint Lucia for several years. At the airport we discussed my coming to Curacao to celebrate my mom's fiftieth birthday the following year. Little did I know that this would be the very last time I would see him alive. A couple of weeks later he was dead, of a massive heart attack.

His funeral was unlike anything I have ever witnessed. It seemed that the whole of Curacao turned out and lined the streets in large numbers to bid farewell to this baseball icon. I had never been aware of the impact that this Saint Lucian had on the psyché of the people of Curacao. I always wondered how my mother was able to survive his sudden death.

After the death of Ernie, she remained in Curacao for the next 14 years but her health was deteriorating. Then in 1996, after many years, I visited Curacao, on the advice of her doctors, friends and neighbours. I spent a week with her before returning to Saint Lucia. The doctors in Curacao had convinced me that it was best to take her home because she was lonely and so I did in 1997. She lived with me for one year in the apartment which I later vacated and did everything I could have done to develop a normal mother and son relationship if that was at all possible, which wasn't easy, as she would go through regular mood swings. Sometimes she would say some of the most outrageous and insensitive things to me.

Most times the subject was my father David Z, which was usually negative and had become a source of bother if not embarrassment to me. It was as though she had never got over him after some forty years and besides that, had remarried in 1963, just a year after the divorce in England. I found it all extremely bizarre to say the least.

Quite often she would invite me to lunch and would enthusiastically cook one of her "Curacaolean" delights. I need not tell you how stuffed I was on leaving the apartment, as she would insist that I ate everything on the plate which was no easy task. However, I really appreciated her kindness and hospitality but it was as though she was trying to make up for the lost years and sometimes tried too hard, instead of allowing things to play out naturally.

The situation was further compounded by a mental health condition which had plagued her right after the sham marriage had officially ended. This condition necessitated constant replenishment of her prescribed medication which I sought to get for her, as not having it created a chemical imbalance which affected her sleep routine at night and made her tired, restless and irritable. I had learnt very early to recognize those symptoms when she didn't take them. Further, she needed someone to administer the dosage to her on a daily basis, as well as to assist in accomplishing some of her household chores and in particular, shopping, cooking, washing and ironing which she loved to do. So I sought the assistance of Veronica, who had been my regular help for some years while residing in the CDC and at DSP. Later, when it seemed that she needed more care than we could have given, I got her admitted to the Marian Home in November, 2006.

My mother Julietta seemed to have settled down quite nicely at the home and was usually alone in her room whenever I visited. Sometimes I would find her mingling with some of the other residents in the outer hall facing the Marchand Grounds especially after breakfast and lunch were served. Mom made friends easily and was definitely a hit with them. I was quite fortunate and blessed to have sat down with her on her birthday on 24th September, 2008. She surprised me by offering a lady who had joined us some KFC, which we followed with a toast with some non alcoholic champagne. The lunchtime session was great fun with lots of laughter and stories about her early years and some things she recollected during the short time spent at the home. It was a rarity to have seen her in this mood and I enjoyed myself immensely, not realizing that this would be the last time that I would have celebrated her birthday with her. So it is in more ways than one, a very special memory.

Around that same period, she was hospitalized a couple of times complaining of stomach aches, but was discharged after a few days on both occasions. On a visit to Victoria Hospital that final time, I made several enquiries about her condition, but no one seemed to really know what her issues were as the x-rays didn't show up anything definitively.

Eventually the doctor advised me that they would be operating on her so he would keep me informed. On the day of the procedure I recall being tense and nervous as the minutes ticked by, and when I didn't hear from Dr. Kabs by 2:00 pm, I mustered the courage to call him fearing the worst. He explained it this way. " I had to stitch her up as quickly as I had opened her Dave. She has pancreatic cancer, Stage 4, and in that condition she doesn't have much time to live, at the most three to four weeks". I was stunned and shocked by this revelation and after receiving further advice from him, began to immediately map out in my mind how I would need to change my work and leisure schedules to facilitate her as much as possible in the coming days.

So it was with a heavy heart that I visited her the following day and did everything possible to look and sound positive. Shortly after my arrival, she would say to me. " Have you seen or heard any news from the doctor? And what has he said to you?" I responded somewhat cautiously, "No! I've not seen him as yet but will do so very soon", but the long, penetrative gaze she flashed was enough to convince me that she knew that I wasn't being truthful. There was very little discussion after that, with the occasional question from her about my work and a little small talk here and there. Standing there at her bedside, I kept hoping that she would open up and share some of the answers I'd been wishing for since her return to Saint Lucia over the last decade or so, but despite her illness, I was touched by her concern for the hard-working nurses on the ward. That was my mother, sometimes bitter, sometimes sweet. I wished that she could have listened more to me. She used to wear me out. She drove me nuts sometimes but she was also big hearted, kind, loving, exuding warmth and had a most generous spirit, a very giving and caring woman. I would sooner forget her sharp tongue and remember her engaging smile and deep concern for humanity.

I felt extremely uncomfortable and emotionally drained and suggested that I would be back to visit her on the following day, but didn't do so, nor the day after, as I was having difficulty coping with the entire episode. I didn't think it was my responsibility to tell my mother that the end was near. What child would do such a thing? My mother's marriage to David Z was obviously a painful experience, so much so she shied away from discussing the details even when I pressed her. Maybe it was my physical appearance that was a constant reminder of the terrible moments that her first marriage was. It was not a nice feeling living under that cloud.

She was discharged that Saturday afternoon and taken back to the Marian Home. There was every indication that she was in a lot of pain and groaning all night into the early morning. On the following Monday, just after midday, I visited the home to discuss her condition with Sister Annie, so as to determine what could be done to minimize her suffering and make her as comfortable as possible. Sister Annie recognized my distress and suggested that I went home, promising to keep me informed about Mom's progress.

So, on leaving her office and walking towards the direction of the car park, I suddenly had this very strong desire to go upstairs to see her. She was lying on the bed in the small room groaning and whimpering very softly. I told her that I was there, and began stroking her brow continuously. I had noticed that some dark stuff was already coming out of her mouth but her eyes were tightly shut. I felt so helpless and in awe of the moment. That once feisty and garrulous woman was in pain and I couldn't do a thing to help her. She suddenly raised her left arm and one of the helpers suggested that my mom was trying to draw attention to the wedding band which she removed from her finger seconds later, then handed it over to me.

I recall stroking her hand for a few moments and within seconds, I heard her breathe her last. I couldn't help but remember that the same spirit which had me to return to Saint Lucia from Barbados, just in time for my Grandmother's passing in 1988, had lured me to spend the final moments with my mother. The general feeling by the staffers at the home was that my Mother struggled to stay alive that weekend, until she heard my voice. It was in my view, a very powerful and indefinable moment that was deserving of mention. Mom passed shortly after 1:00 pm that Monday, 4th May, 2009, at the age of 75 years.

Shortly after Mom passed, I immediately contacted Darnell (my Uncle) to seek his advice about funeral arrangements and really appreciated his guidance and assistance during this extremely difficult time. Fortunately, Carlyle, my other Uncle was in Saint Lucia from the US on vacation, attending the annual Saint Lucia Jazz Festival. Both of them had been regular visitors at the Marian Home, as well as during her years residing in the CDC. She always recounted to me the wonderful visits, particularly when Uncle Carlyle was present and how much she had missed her sisters Marcia and Maria who had both passed some years earlier. She was particularly fond of Maria's daughters Maran and Shelly.

A few days before the funeral, while rummaging through some of her belongings, I came across a letter penned by her. It formed part of the eulogy which I delivered at her funeral. Here is an excerpt which really helps to put her life and indeed, mine, into some perspective.

In her very own words:

I was brought up by a single parent mother. She was a seamstress. What a treasure. She was the very best. She had such high Godly principles and morals. She taught me much and did all that she could to make me happy. In fact, she spoiled me. I, on the other hand, was headstrong.

After leaving school, I trained to become a nurse but did not continue because I was filled with wanting my own way. My vision was blurred. My mom was there, or so I thought. I had nothing to worry about. But I soon realized that life does have its ups and downs. All kinds of episodes crowded my life. I learnt that life was not all cream.

I got married at 17 years. We had a son, David, the only one I've got. I had such high hopes for him and his father, but after three years, his father left for England. The marriage was a sham. A surge of hard knocks followed. I was devastated and horrified. My life became scarred, and my morals became marred. I was so unhappy. I drew away from my mother's teachings. "Marriage in name only", she said, "is no marriage at all." I had to get out of this mess, so I left for the U.K. to seek a divorce.

I believed that the Lord's hand was upon me because of disobedience, but I couldn't see the light then. Unhappiness and anguish trailed after me. I sought release from my problems, moved from England to Curacao, and married again. Life was better with my second husband. He was my soul mate. He was kind and easy-going and made up for all that I had lacked. He took care of my every need. We were not rich but comfortable. He was a household name in the Dutch Antilles because of his involvement in baseball, especially his management of training and devotion to the next generation of baseball players. Ernie travelled all over the Americas to officiate at international games as an umpire. I was so proud of him…the passion he had for the game, the respect he had earned from young and old alike in the Antilles was tremendous. As he went to his games, at home and abroad, I turned more and more to the Lord, leading me on, day after day, every hour, by the minute. He never gives up on us if we seek him.

Then the shock. September 4, 1982 my husband had a massive heart attack and died. My life was torn and I thought I could not go on, but the Lord said I could. I learned much the hard-way, peace in the raging storm. Many a night I cried myself to sleep and I'd say, "the cup is bitter, Lord, but I'll drink it. Just be by my side and never leave me" and I felt that it was so.

Now, my bible has become my compass because it is God's word that feeds us and makes life worthwhile, for it speaks of Him, our one and only savior, Jesus Christ, God the Father and Holy Spirit who directs us and leads us into all truth. During my life's journey, I've proven time and time again that once God is the wind beneath your wings, you do not have to be afraid of the challenges of life.

"Marcienne Julietta Smith"

Sometime during mid August, 2017, I was fortunate to run into this bubbly, middle aged lady, now a retired civil servant, who at the time that mom was alive had recounted some of her experiences while visiting the Marian Home to see her Father and two Aunts who were resident there. So I grabbed the opportunity to find out what were some of the memories she had of my mom. She described the occasional meetings this way. .

"I can't say precisely what drew me to your mother, but something did. I remember her direct gaze and openness to conversation and trusting me with precious family memorabilia, black and white photos, other important documents and her wanting to share stories of her early life." And she continued with this dramatic statement; "She was particularly regretful of being out of her son's life and did not believe that he had forgiven her for the abandonment, but I found her sophisticated and ahead of women her age group, in that she was open to engaging conversation with younger women on current issues. She was definitely a presence in the home and had a quick smile and sense of humor" concluded our civil servant retiree. ..

Other reactions have also come from Sister Annie Reneau-Administrator of the Marian Home, and some of the caregivers. The edited statement from the administrator follows:

Being in such an institution, one's privacy is often compromised and adaptability becomes the order of the day. An elder either surrenders by way of acceptance or defies all odds to preserve their independence.

Julietta Smith was reserved, yet very jovial and friendly and found peace within the walls of the Marian Home. Her room became the inner space where she would entertain those thoughts which were generally pleasant, as she often smiled sitting in her chair in her semi dark room. Julietta often welcomed visitors, friends and her caregivers with a warm, contagious smile, and the look on her face was often difficult to interpret, yet her smile sucked you in..

She nurtured a relationship with the staff who became her extended family, who at the same time appreciated her independence. She usually rewarded staff and persons whose services she sought, whether it was the laundress Diana Albert, who also did her banking transactions and other personal errands, or her hair stylist, who would come to her room while she would direct the styling to her satisfaction.

She was sensitive to and appreciative of all the extras that were done for her, and so she felt that monetary reward was necessary, even when she was informed that she didn't have to pay those individuals for their services. She was appreciative of the staff who cared for her and treated them with respect. She was caring, always giving advice and shared stories about her own life and how and why she had left Saint Lucia.

Julietta kept abreast with current issues and was often found listening to her transistor radio, after all, her son David was often on and maybe it gave her the opportunity to get to know him better, and exposed her to the other side of Dave. In my conversations and whenever Dave was the subject, she was often very tactful and reserved her opinion, and though she didn't appear to openly express much affection, she was certainly proud of him.

After some five years or so of keeping in touch via email and social media, Bettina and Peter, her husband, finally arrive in Saint Lucia for a two week vacation on Thursday 1st March but we didn't meet until Saturday,10th March, 2018, when I organized a day cruise for them along the island's west coast on the catamaran, "Queen of the Carnival", past the quaint fishing villages of Anse La Raye and Canaries, dotting the lush, verdant green landscape, world famous Anse Chastanet hotel with its stunning deep sea diving and right next door, the Internationally Acclaimed and Breathtaking", Jade Mountain" Resort, the "creme de la creme" in Saint Lucian hospitality. We then moved into the Picturesque town of Soufriere with its Majestic Pitons, dubbed World Heritage status since 2004. The Botanical Gardens visit really rekindled in me an appreciation for Saint Lucia's rich and diverse flora and fauna. It was so good to have seen my guests utilizing the therapeutic qualities of the mineral baths at the drive-in volcano landmark and words cannot aptly describe the gastronomic delight that was lunch at the Fond Doux Plantation. Then later, stops at Anse Cochon for snorkellng and swimming and then cruise into idyllic Marigot Bay with its panoramic Yacht Haven Marina before returning to Ganter's Bay in Castries. Wow! What a delightful day! The trip really made me realize what a stunningly, beautiful country Saint Lucia is. When you are mired down in work 24/7, it's so easy to deprive yourself of leisure and some well deserved fun. This is how Bettina describes the day via whatsapp, the following day. " Dave, thank you so much for that wonderful cruise on that fantastic ship. This day will definitely stay forever in our hearts". That's what my country, Saint Lucia, does to every visitor, even a sister residing on the other side of the World. Nuff said!

CHAPTER 8

MR. CHAIRMAN

There was nothing they wanted, nothing I could give them,
but this thing I have called "The Light of the World." (Derek
Walcott – Nobel Laureate for Literature, 1992)

As already indicated, I was taken off the air at RSL when the SLP returned to power in 2011, and was informed of this in January 2012, by the Ministry of Information under its garrulous minister, Dr. Jimmy Fletcher, and if I were to recall what occurred on that Wednesday morning during Coffee Break at Sandals Halcyon, when PM Anthony was my guest mere days before the 2006 General Election, I shouldn't have been too surprised because of the many stories being circulated that if anyone crossed "The Chief" they would have to pay!

Those of you who've followed my broadcasting career would know that my main goal is to try always to disseminate accurate information to the general public, and the political persuasion of my guests never mattered as demonstrated time and time again by the frequent SLP guests invited to appear on The Agenda during Prime Minister King's UWP administration and so Harold Dalson, Philip J. Pierre, Dr. Robert Lewis usually along with Jeannine (who had by then resigned from the UWP) were fairly regular guests, but I also interviewed Alva Baptiste, Dr. Desmond Long and others and encouraged callers within their camp like Mr. Moses "Musa" JnBaptiste, Vieux Fort North MP, Tom Walcott, Salty, one of the chief campaigners for Dr. Anthony as well as some Flambeau surrogates. So, imagine my dismay that genuine efforts to balance the partisan rhetoric, was not generally appreciated by the power brokers in the governing party after the elections of 2011.

Calabash management wanted me to replicate the radio version of "The Agenda" and it was agreed that the program would be called "Mr. Chairman". The show was launched during the first quarter of 2013 and was greeted enthusiastically by the public, although it took me a while to become used to the cameras again, after having done only radio consistently for the past 10 years, the last TV show being "Tourism is our Business" throughout the mid 90's, but so much had changed since and I wasn't sure that I was capable, far less ready to transition into TV again.

What also concerned me most in my new role was the challenge, not to get bored or be boring. I didn't want merely to have live studio guests, but to produce a program with cutaways, inserts, clips, vox pops and video of actual live events, which would have differentiated us from our competitors. I discussed it all with the management, but one year later, then two, three and now four, not much has happened despite follow up meetings. I finally came to the realization that my best efforts to lace the program with all of the above to enhance its content was not a priority, not that it didn't occur occasionally, but the consistency was lacking due to other pressing matters that my producer and cameraman had to attend to. You can well imagine the frustration I underwent... Then we saw the return of Rick Wayne on DBS and "Can I help You?" with Richard Frederick on MBC, on the very same night and time that Mr. Chairman is broadcast. There's no doubt that many viewers are lured by Richard's penchant for explosive revelations, some embarrassingly so, week after week and Rick's hard hitting, researched expose' that appears to be "A thorn" in the SLP camp, but no one can ever be sure which Rick shows up on a Thursday so Rick has earned his stripes and to my knowledge has never said anything that hasn't been thoroughly researched. Supporters of both sides await with baited breaths what emanates from his STINGING TALK. Hence it is competitive and it really depends on how strongly aligned you are to the existing parties, for I really don't see supporters of the UWP tuning in to

Frederick, given his history with the party leader, unless out of curiosity sometimes.

Mr. Chairman has always been more interview oriented rather than what some have described as "Bully Pulpit" driven. There are some people out there who love the juicy tidbits, and there are others who don't and they express that opinion and so like a restaurant that offers you a menu, you are given a choice to make. Many view us on Thursdays, but I know that thousands more view the rebroadcast on Sundays and during the week, all because of the many choices on Thursdays.

Also, and because I was always constantly wanting to experiment, I suggested to management the production of a tourism program, because it is still my opinion that not enough is being done by the government and the stakeholders to inform and educate the masses about an industry that is now being described as the country's number one economic earner. Also suggested some four years ago the start of morning programming which interestingly a couple of TV stations have started and they must be given credit for taking this bold step. I encouraged management to look at the possibility of a program that would focus on the biographies of many of our sons and daughters, some of whom have passed on, with little or no fanfare. It saddens me that even that suggestion hasn't materialized, which has really made me miss the control that I had at DSP, for I would have zeroed in on those three projects with their amazing potential.

Sadly a number of icons are passing on and we don't have any record on file of their many achievements and the impact they have made on the society. I'm even more saddened because I was regularly in touch with three of the recent dead--Justice Suzie d'Auvergne, Mr. Dunstan Fontenelle and Chef Harry.

I thought I had time (Suzie, Chef, Fonty) but how wrong I was. To make it an effective production, we could utilize any photographs/videos they may have compiled and in some instances speak to some of those (on camera) who are familiar with them personally and professionally.

Something needs to be done, so that generations now and to come, will learn about Saint Lucia's history and the many people and events that shaped it.

Here's a short list of potential interviewees:

Ms Joyce Auguste (Music/Netball)
Mrs Paula Calderon (Business)
Winston Hinkson (Broadcasting)
Jeff Fedee (Broadcasting)
Harold George (B/cast Technician)
Rameau Poleon (Musician)
Hollis Bristol (Business/Politics)
Ira D'Auvergne (Law/Politics)
Kenneth Monplaisir (Law)
Arthur Jacobs (Crafts/Actor)
Lucille Fontenelle (Public Servant)
Dr. Winston Paris (Medicine)
Dunstan Du Boulay (Business)
Ms Alicia John (School Teacher)
Dr. Vaughan Lewis (Former PM)
Mr. Fred Devaux (Business)
Ms Ingrid Skerrit (Business)
Ms Emelda Charles (Broadcaster)
Mr. Charles Cadet (Former Diplomat/Musician)
Mr. Neville Cenac (Former MP)

Now let us get back to Mr. Chairman.

There has been a feeling in some circles that the program was advancing the cause of the UWP, and those who've come to that conclusion would not have understood the innumerable efforts on my part to invite many of the same persons who were regulars on the Agenda while in opposition. It was usually an exercise in futility as Dalson and others were always promising to show up, but it was always the same, "We'll call you back", "Call us next week" or "Will be off island." Gratefully some have responded. Also, we've noted a plethora of programs hosted by party surrogates on electronic media which to my mind is a very ineffective move as they only attract the party's base and not supporters of the other party or those who see themselves as "Independents or the floating voters"

In my view party officials should really try to avoid the monopolization of the airwaves by themselves and party hacks. It turns people off as you hear the same people regurgitating the same topics on three - four talk shows daily. Also you should advise your callers to be courteous and respectful to the host who's just trying to do his/her job as professionally as possible. Because there are established rules, guidelines and protocols, I've been described by some partisans as biased, but I'll continue to do my very best conscientiously until I can't do it anymore.

The following are some thoughts about the island's political landscape as articulated on Mr. Chairman from time to time. The 1997 (16-1) SLP mandate was an astounding result, but in my view, not entirely surprising for the following reasons.

- The UWP's "Messiah JC" had retired in 1996.
- Dr. Lewis, his hand chosen successor created a split within the UWP camp.
- After winning the safe Castries Central Seat, Dr. Lewis should have called a snap General Election within one or two months of his Prime Ministership.
- A reorganized SLP, brought in Dr. Anthony as its new leader.
- The re-admission of Odlum served to unite the Labour forces which had been divided since 1982, when the then SLP Government collapsed.
- Odlum singlehandedly decapitated the political ambitions of Dr. Lewis with his "*Toujou Sou*" (habitually drunk) platform rhetoric and theatrics.
- The UWP's poor mobilization, days before the election, was demoralizing to their base and a turn off to potential new voters.
- The UWP's anti SLP television commercials backfired.

It is still my view that anyone leading the SLP would have won. Clearly it was Julian Hunte's time, but with him out of the picture, the electorate saw Kenny Anthony as the new messiah. His name had been touted for a few years but that resounding 1997 mandate would not have been possible without Odlum.

By 2001, The Saint Lucia Labour party lost 10,000 votes from 44,153 to 34, 142 votes, which was extremely significant and while the UWP was thrashed 14-3, it was clear that the break up of the Alliance with Sir John, Odlum and Dr. Morella Joseph at the helm, had threatened to undermine the SLP's stranglehold on the electorate, which was the reason KDA sought a new mandate in December, 2001, six months before it was constitutionally due. Interestingly, the UWP lost 3000 votes which I've put down to voter apathy towards the new leadership of the UWP and with disappointment in the Alliance breakup.

In 2005, when Sir John announced his intention to come out of retirement to lead the UWP once again, I heard the bell tolling for KDA, and I was proven right. In the 2006 General Elections, the UWP received 38,894 votes, a whopping increase of nearly 15,000 votes over their 2001 tally of 23, 095, while the SLP increased to 36, 604 votes from 34,142. It was always a great source of amusement to me whenever Philip J. was my guest during that period. He would only refer to the 2000 plus votes, which was the UWP winning margin. The significant development though, was that Sir John had defied the pundits and overturned the KDA (14-3) landslide to a UWP (11-6) astounding victory.

Nevertheless it's to the credit of the SLP that 5 years later, they were able to regain power in the election of 2011. SLP-42, 640 to UWP's 39,336 votes - An 11-6 mandate.

Here are 10 Reasons why UWP lost...

1. Sir John died in 2007. His supporters were not committed to King, his successor, and stayed away.
2. Many believed the SLP propaganda that some in the UWP, were responsible for Sir John's death...

3. Supporters were also aware of the Compton family's distrust of some of King's cabinet members...

4. Like sitting ducks, UWP allowed the SLP machinery and social media to define them, with little or no response.

5. There were at least 5 UWP (MP's) that the party faithful wanted to see step down.

6. The launch of the party manifesto was delayed, lack lustre, unlike the hype of 2006.

7. Mysteriously, the UWP held no major rallies or activities during the final week of the poll.

8. The SLP polling station personnel were better organized and more aggressive in getting their supporters to vote.

9. Most people viewed PM King as a nice guy, but were unimpressed with his leadership.

10. Perhaps more importantly, the much debated Sir John monument was not going to be installed by his party prior to the General Elections.

Fast Forward June 6, 2016.

From the very inception 2013-2016, the SLP used the same tactics that defeated King against new party leader Allen Chastanet. The barrage of negative UWP TV commercials and anti Chastanet rhetoric went on unabated throughout these years, but it didn't work. On the contrary the electorate gave Chastanet a stunning mandate, making him the only UWP leader since Sir John to be successful at the polls.

UWP--46, 183
SLP---37,148

A surprising 7% swing to his party with another 11-6 mandate, winning the General Election by over 9,000 votes. Truly an amazing feat for a newcomer who stood up to everything that was hurled at him from the other side.

From (2013 2016) Mr. Chairman was usually politically charged in a manner that I've never experienced before. The insults, arguments and disrespect demonstrated by some callers towards the host and his guests with contrasting viewpoints were just 'unacceptable' and must be discouraged. As a national, I felt embarrassed and ashamed at the level that some callers had sunk to. Callers should not think that they have the right to call a show and to speak as long as they want and when the host is forced to end the diatribe, they would hurl a sling of abuses at him and many friends in the Diaspora speak of the outrage they felt when they listened to what passes for discussion on the airwaves. I've played my part in trying to differentiate between my show and some of the others, and have had some tough times simply because I would not engage some callers at their level.

That period was quite a challenge, particularly when the politicians were on. My grateful thanks to Randall with whom I've had the pleasure to work with since the program's inception and the respect and courtesy he's demonstrated to myself and the many who were seated opposite me on the set. They have always remarked on how conscientious and respectful he's been; he's really "One of a Kind."

I've presented well over 200 Mr. Chairman programs on Calabash Television from 2013-2017. A large number of those have been with politicians and their surrogates, public servants, Police and Emergency Services administrators, Health and Tourism personnel, Musicians, Calypsonians, their writers and with several youth organizations including officials of the National Youth Council (NYC). I've really enjoyed them all and the most impactful of all the programs have been 3 in particular: Jason Sifflet, Kenita Placide and the most talked about has been Sam *"Juk Bois"* Flood as he commemorated 40 years of Kweyol broadcasts in Saint Lucia. The program was first broadcast on September 4, 2014.

The Jason Sifflet appearance was promoted this way: "Here's a guy who's kicking lots of butts on social media and I'm speaking here of the Flogg Blogger himself. Some see dat rastaman as a villain and dangerous, while others as a pot smoking crazy dude" His controversial views on our politicians were generally regarded as wild claims but no one can deny his brilliantly written pieces which usually contained a lot of expletives. The way Jason puts it "There are desperate efforts by some out there to silence me and I've even got empirical evidence that there's a "Hit" on my life, as well as a couple of others in the media fraternity like Tim Poleon and Clinton Reynolds" As a result he announced the discontinuation of the Blogg. It was a night of shocking revelations and there was actually a moment on the set when I thought that Jason wanted to unseat me as host. Such was the impact of his gesticulations as he inched menacingly towards me. The show created quite a buzz, so much so, he returned a few weeks later.

Ms Kenita Placide makes a strong case for the LBGT population through her Organization "United and Strong Inc", and the several hindrances facing them. Kenita shared distraught stories about the number of gay people in Saint Lucia who had been murdered, some brutally, while others have been victims of violence and discrimination because of their lifestyle, and the interventions being taken by her organization to educate and inform the general public about some of those issues. She also cautioned "Gays" not to fall into some of the traps that were being set out for them, either by those who took violent reprisals against them, as well as some who were on the down low, afraid to come out due to marital or social obligations and gays or bisexuals who were courting those "status symbols" were perhaps unaware that some of those people are liable to commit murder so as to retain their anonymity. Some of these people would be out cruising late nights/wee morning hours seeking same sex encounters, particularly in the islands north with its restaurants, bars and entertainment spots. This was definitely an eye opener. In May 2017, Bennet Charles, the Communications and Advocacy Officer was my guest on the programme, highlighting some of the bold projects and activities being undertaken by the organization to have their members protect themselves from loose sexual behavior.

Sam "Juk Bois" Flood: Undoubtedly the islands foremost Kweyol broadcaster and arguably the most listened to on radio today. He's appeared every year and responds to questions in English, much to the surprise of some and amusement of most viewers. Listening to him roll his 'R's' provides much light-hearted fun. I don't think that any other guest has received as many calls of greetings and commendations as does Sam. It is as though the country comes to a standstill, to listen and view what he has to say and he revels in it with his signature hat and broad smile.

One learnt that he began his broadcasting career in 1974 on Radio Caribbean International (RCI) with *"Radio Say San Nous"* every evening except Sundays from 7:30 until 9pm, and on the occasion of the 40th Anniversary he appeared with Earl Huntley, the man credited with introducing him to radio, and after a somewhat rocky start, really gave rural Saint Lucia a voice that it had never had before and the broadcasting landscape has never been the same since.

On that milestone evening I presented him with a cake, the four and the zero being candles, which he blew before his adoring fans. We also sipped on some champagne to toast the occasion and I thought I may have detected him trying to hold back a few tears, such was the emotion of the moment. I have no doubt that all who viewed were tremendously moved. Sam was back on with me in early November, 2017, and we had among other items, an extremely animated discussion about the recently organized *"Jounen Kweyol"* activities in the four communities of Belle Vue-Vieux Fort, Dennery, Marigot and Babonneau, which culminated activities as part of October's Kweyol Heritage Month.

Says *"Juk Bois,"* "A great deal more needs to be done by Paba's Folk Research Center, (FRC) "to promote the educational and social components of the "Old Kweyol Way", that were part of the day to day lives of our parents and grandparents". He also noted that most of the foods available for sale were being prepared a day or so before the event, which to him did not compliment what the day should be. "I would like to see most of our foods prepared on the Sunday and as much as possible in the presence of customers. It is also important that some effort be made by the FRC to honor those who have made tremendous contributions to the advancement of our Kweyolness" and to Saint Lucia's Folk Culture, he singled out the late Vocalist/Drummer Eric Adley and Musician and Choir Mistress, Joyce Auguste. "I am at a loss to understand why an honor has not been bestowed on those two individuals up to now", he emphasized.

Finally, he gave us an amazing story about his primary school days in Vieux Fort, where it seemed that speaking Kweyol was strictly forbidden, which in some way was connected to the British authorities, as we were then one of their many colonies. Because they couldn't understand the language, they did everything to discourage its use, (perhaps in fear of a mutiny). *"Juk Bois"* said that he, along with others, were physically punished with a thick strap for doing so in the classroom, or at anytime the school monitors reported the speaking of Kweyol to and from school by the students, so he quipped, "I got a lot of licks, but I took it all in stride because I knew that some day, in the not too distant future, it would be worth it. A country that doesn't acknowledge its culture is dead. That is why for me *Jounen Kweyol* is not just a day in the month of October, but every day of the year". A very powerful endorsement on Mr. Chairman, from undoubtedly the most popular guest on the program, Sam *"Juk Bois"* Flood.

One of the embarrassing moments about being a "Live" program host are the very late starts, which was never an issue on the Agenda at RSL where we always began at 8:30am promptly. However, late starts seem to be "normal" at Calabash. I was usually at great pains to respond to the queries of my invited guests already seated opposite me on the set. "Mr. Chairman!, what time do we start?", I would respond, "In a short while", trying very hard to conceal my embarrassment.

This was usually indicated by several other viewers whom I would run into on the streets or at a social event, who would ask, "did you have a show on Thursday?", I would respond, "Yes!", and they would continue, "well, we kept tuning in up to 8:50pm and even after that and still no start, not even a message to inform viewers to stay tuned for the program, so we selected some other channels whose shows were already in progress", my usual response, "well! You can always view the repeat broadcast on Sunday you know", always hoping that they wouldn't ask me much more after that response, as I've always had difficulty in responding to matters that I've had no control over.

One final note. Producers must learn not to take the viewing public for granted and just as importantly the guests, hosts and sponsors too, against the backdrop of the fierce competition that is so evident in the media landscape today. They should also come to the realization that they can't do it all alone and should seek to employ the requisite numbers required to do the job, otherwise quality will be compromised. It may be better to produce and present fewer programs and do them very well, rather than do too many partially well. I might add that this approach has always befuddled me.

From top- left to right..

* Hosting Live! RSL's "The Agenda"2011* Dave at 30 something?* Mom in 2007* Sir John at Skyview Map function (85)* An award from Sir John on the occasion of 10th Independence Anniversary-89* Copy of Woy Album presented to a young Stephenson King and Louis George in 87(both Government Ministers)* Mom and I at Ernie's funeral in Curacao-82* Partying at "Sparrow Gold" in 2005* Grandmother(mom about 10 yrs old)* After receiving slmm award at GHouse* After award with Uncle Darnell and Wife-Sybil-2017* DSP banner at St. Lucia video launch-91* A young Grand mother* Mom at 40 yrs? (Mid 70's)* Dave in his 30's holidaying in LA-86* Dame Pearlette offers congratulations after pinning award-2017* David Z in the mid 70's in Germany* Map presentation to Cunard La Toc General Manager 85* After Award with Winall/Christine at GH* Finally, Dave in his 20's

Plaque presentation by Minister Lansiquot to DS

At age 8 years old

At RCI in the late 60's

At RSL in the early 70's

At around 25 years old

Granny on her way to church

Mom

The Eyes Have It!

At Black Tie Event in Canada

Close up

Photos by Dunstan Martial

On leaving Soufriere (World Famous Pitons).

Cruising at Marigot

Photos by Dunstan Martial

CHAPTER 9

DEAR CALYPSO

"Calypso is about life and a reflection of the society, things
that are happening here and in the world".
(Sparrow — Calypso King of the World, right after the 1985 competition)

Dear Calypso-Ah feel is time dat I let you know
Before you finally leave an go, an we ain't have you more
Dear Calypso-In our culture an our heart
You play a very important part, so why do we disrespect you like dat

Just a part of a verse from Pelay's "Dear Calypso" which we've used as the title of the chapter and a fitting tribute to him, who's captured the monarchy six times in his illustrious 40 year career, winning consecutively 1969-1972, 1978 and 2003, the road march title twice and the Soca competition once.

As a teenager growing up, Pelay was easily my role model and that of others in the CDC area. He was my neighbor and lived with his Grandmother Ma Na, (my grandmother was Miss Na) at Block W, Apt 16, just downstairs of where I resided. He would be at rehearsals about three evenings weekly with the Big Six Orchestra, at the home of Johnson, a band member. I can still hear the musical strains emanating from Coral Street with the fleet fingered Augustus "Pan" Andrew on keyboards. That's how my appreciation for music was fed, and the love of Saint Lucian Calypso began through Pelay, during his early years in the artform.

In 1971, Pelay became the first calypsonian to record on 45rpm and two years later recorded a full Christmas long playing album which has brought so much nostalgia and joy to Saint Lucians at home and in the Diaspora, particularly with the tracks "Christmas Saint Lucian style" and *"Sey Tradition Nwel"*. However, he was best known for his slow and melodious commentary and his witty and hard hitting political satire.

MERRY CHRISTMAS - (St. Lucian Style - Pelay)

Verse 1   *Music in de air, an' people everywhere*
Are wishing you good cheer
So come on everyone, it's time we had some fun
The Jolly Christmas Season has begun.

Chorus: **(And leh me wish you) Merry Christmas, Merry Christmas,**
St. Lucian Style, It's de only place I know
Where people celebrate so
De Birth of De Holy Child.

Verse 2:   *After Midnight Mass, when fete start to blast*
Make sure you have enough liquor to last
Cause dat's de time of year, when old friends suddenly appear
An' they'll drink wit you until the next new year.

Verse 3:   *As a Saint Lucian, I'm telling you as man*
Christmas here is a special occasion
We doh have no snow, an' the mistletoe we doh know
But when it comes to fete we lead the show.

Verse 4:   *See de old an' young, feting all around*
Ah tell yuh man Christmas here is right on
So if you are down here, you'll love dis time of year
Just come along we've got a drink to spare.

Up until his death in 2011 at the age of 67 years, it is said that he'd composed about 350 songs of which 135 were personally recorded on at least 23 records, tapes and CD's. Another 40 songs have been recorded by other artistes like Lady Leen, Jackson, Sac Papier, and Lord Believe Me among others.

Pelay was extremely disciplined, a perfect gentleman and very shewed about his entertainment business. He was outspoken on calypso and copyright matters and was always insisting on accountability from the association and HMS now ECCO. Pelay was a tough, no nonsense kind of guy. His love of country was undeniable and one of the few persons known to place the Saint Lucian flag outside of his home during Independence celebrations. He even requested to be buried in a yellow shirt and a bow tie depicting the flag. Pelay is also credited for penning the National Pledge.

In the arena, Pelay considered both Pep and Invader as his main rivals but admired Pep greatly. He felt that Invader was too deeply entrenched in politics as a calypsonian and that is why, whenever Invader recorded a pro-labour song, he would record one for the UWP, and would use a lot of picong in his lyrics.

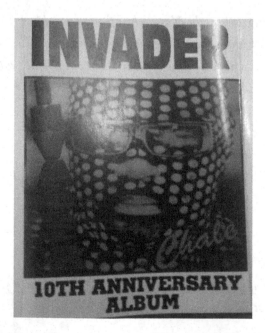

His manager Ian Sanchez told me that despite being differently abled as a result of a car crash in 1972 in the USA, Pelay was able to get Saint Lucians to have respect for people with disabilities and if anything, Sanchez feels that it may have spurred him on to excel at the highest level.

I've done quite a bit in promoting and financing the artform in a huge way in the past. First in 1988 with the production of the "Woy" album featuring Pep, Invader, Educator, Tricky, Short pants, Kneah and Chippy and the "King - Ashanti, the Dread - Herb Black and Buffalo" in 1991, and Invader's 1993, 10th Anniversary album, which featured tracks like "*Kole*", "*Vye Nohm Sala*", "Pussy Cat" and "Ring de Iron".

I've always loved calypso from a little boy growing up and recognized the impact it's had in addressing the myriad issues in a direct and unfiltered way and in the process, the play on the psyché of not just the fans and others in the community, but on the movers and shakers at the political and economic level in the country.

We've been fortunate to have had the likes of Pelay, Jackson, Invader, Pep, Ashanti, Educator, Herb Black, Morgie, Wally, Mr. Brown, Bingo, Lady Leen and Lady Spice for many seasons, not forgetting Jany who tragically passed away a few weeks after capturing the monarchy in 2004. I had interviewed her on "Coffee Break at Sandals" just days before. Mention here of the incredible consistency of Menell, Nintus and Journalist and the super talented newcomers: Solange, Ready, Lil Nick and Qshun who've inspired many and whom we hope will be around for many seasons.

On October 2nd, 2011, RSL 97 presented the "Monarchs" at Pointe Seraphine. The show was initiated and organized by myself with the assistance of a small working committee, including station manager, Mary Polius. The Monarchs headlined Menell who was reigning at the time, along with Invader and Ricky T, with a guest appearance by Barbados' 9 time Monarch "The Mighty Gabby".

What I had attempted to do, was to have the performers go through a sort of cabaret set for about 45 minutes each. They would speak to the audience between numbers and perform a repertoire which had brought them fame, success and lots of airplay. The show was unique and successfully presented. The festivals band did a wonderful job accompanying them but the turn out left a lot to be desired, mainly due to several competing events that October weekend, especially Octobre Fest En Kweyol organized by WLBL and since we were in an election cycle, a UWP rally in the Dennery North constituency. I had tried my very best, pleading with PM King to postpone the rally to a later date but without success.

Ultimately, my goal was to stage the Monarch annually, to raise the profile of RSL, while providing additional revenue streams, increased advertising dollars, as well as provide income for Calypsonians, Musicians, Sound and Lighting technicians and to give the artistes and their fans a "Classy" Show, merely 10 weeks after the staging of the Calypso finals-one of the main carnival events of the year. Hopefully, that initiative will become a reality sometime in the future, outside of the traditional kaiso season.

In 2017, The Mighty Pep (Dr. Desmond Long) captured the calypso monarchy for the 8th time since his entry into the arena in 1987, fresh out of the University of the West Indies (UWI) Cave Hill Campus, where he had won the annual calypso competition there for 3 consecutive years, 1983, 1984 and 1985, following his only win in 1978 at the St. Mary's College, while a student at that institution.

He describes his relationship with his writer as a great marriage "Rowan is a wordsmith, which suits my moods and music. What most people aren't aware of, is that quite apart from winning an 8th time, we've had 14 first runner's up, which is nothing short of extraordinary over the last 30 years, so the marriage has been one hell of a success". Pep indicated that his first love at the time was pop music and he was part of a group, 'The Petals', but only went into kaiso because of the huge interest in the artform with the emergence of people like Invader, who was on a roll, winning in 1985 and 1986. "I posed a serious challenge to him in 1987, during the finals at the Gaiety Cinema, when I won with 'Learn from them' and 'Unborn child' which is to date the most popular song I've ever sung"

Unborn Child Lyrics

<u>*Verse 1*</u>

In my mother's womb, waiting for my time
I can sense the turmoil going through her mind
Should she keep this child, child not meant to be
Considered a bastard by society.
Who will see things through my eyes?
Ohh...Who will plead my case?
I want to share the beauty, of nature's scenery
I want to claim my right to take my place
And be part of humanity

<u>*Chorus*</u>

Listen to my plea
Show some sympathy
Though I'm not yet born, I have feelings like everyone
Vibrations of life
Filters to my soul
Will I get a chance to be a person in this world?

<u>*Verse 2*</u>

Child without a face, child without a name
Destined for destruction, like a vicious game
Never to enjoy, mother's loving smile
Never even granted the privilege to cry

Dear mother can't you feel me,
Clinging on for sweet life?
Why can't my helpless heartbeat, touch on your tender love?
I want to share the joys of life that comes from our good God above

<u>Verse 3</u>

The abortionist, knocks on mother's door
Seeking one more victim, for his evil claws
Father can't be found, cause he does not care
Mother feels the pressure, fetus feels the fear
Please mother don't surrender
This precious life that you bear
Don't you know life is sacred?
Why can't you understand?
Don't you know pregnancy can never be a mistake in nature's plan

(Repeat Chorus)

Pep recalls the period 1987-1995, which saw great rivalry between the camps of Invader, Ashanti and his own, especially Ashanti, who was being dubbed the *"Malaway* King" winning consecutively in 1990 and 1991. "I was under a lot of pressure in 1992 to disrupt his winning streak. You see, for some unknown reason I was looked upon as the one with upper class support, with Invader, a mixed bag of Malaway and upper class. I got a lot of flack but didn't allow it to railroad me and went on to win the crown that year and later went overseas to study medicine. Invader won the crown in 1993. I returned to compete in 1994, and won the crown. I was under the impression that my study leave had a dramatic impact on my winning.

En Bas Gorge

<u>Verse 1</u>

I'm a Lucian, I'm a true son
And my heart is filled with national pride
But believe me

How it grieves me
When I see us push our Culture aside
I've travelled the region
I've been far away
And in my opinion
I am proud to say
No land, no place, no people, no race
Can match the class of our National heritage

<u>*Chorus*</u>

The time has come for us to savour
The sweetness of Saint Lucian Culture
The richness, and the pleasure
English, French and African
Combined to give the true Saint Lucian flavour
Of the En Bas Gorge La......
Jouer En Bas Gorge La Jouer.... (Repeat)
Jouer, Jouer, Jouer.......Jouer....

<u>*Verse 2*</u>

While in motion, on an excursion
To the countryside nearby Millet
I was greeted, expertly treated
An experience I'll never forget
En Bas Gorge musicians
With percussion parts
The greatest exponents
Of this unique art
They played their strings and made my spirit sing
With pride, a feeling deep down inside

Pep views 2017 as a great season, but is concerned with the management, structure and function of the association and asserted "There is too much reliance on the Government. They have to rethink the way forward and get back on track at the soonest for the survival of the artform."

In response to a question about whom he feels most threatened by on the night of the competition, Pep quipped "I really don't feel threatened by any of them, except for Menell with her great vocal ability and the vibrancy she demonstrates on stage and behind her the prolific compositions of Nahum is always cause for concern as a competitor". In response to the infiltration of political surrogates writing and attempting to influence the goings on during the season he said," Rather than focus on anti-government or anti party songs, the calypsonian needs to bear in mind that hard hitting political songs will never win you the crown. Sing social commentary, hit at the social ills in the society and that has always been my strategy. If you can master these, then you will do very well. You must also keep in mind too the possible biases of the judges, so that mistake could prove disastrous and should be avoided. However, it will obviously be for many, great entertainment during the tents".

Pep continues to be surprised by some calypsonians and their lack of understanding and studying of the criteria; Lyrics, Music and Performance, which is responsible for their lack of success in the competition and it is something that his team pays a lot of attention to. He also said that it was important for him not to peak too early. "When I'm 3rd or even 4th during the preliminaries, I feel comfortable as it gives me the opportunity to recognize where I've fallen short and so I devote the time to sharpening up any weaknesses, based on the criteria set out" advises Pep.

In conclusion he was happy to see the emergence of fresh new barbs like Solange, Ready, Qshun, Lil Nick etc. and feels that the artform is in good hands but with the encouragement, support and guidance of the association, the sponsors and the general public including the media. Those sentiments were also echoed by Nahum who feels that there's a flicker of hope for the artform. Pep also feels that the Sab is the best venue to date. "There wasn't the usual echo which was evident at past venues. Many in the crowd heard us very clearly which added to our confidence. In addition the management of the dressing room facilities backstage was just phenomenal. It was a huge departure from the past and the authorities must be commended for that," said Pep. Here is an excerpt of his composition, "Why I Died," which won him the 2017 monarchy.

WHY I DIED

Verse 1

I Travelled the world, Making fame in places untold
Spreading Lucian literature, to world leaders around the globe
When they took their stand, and made me their Nobel Prized Man
It was a worldwide victory of respect for this Lucian Land
But back here at home most of us just don't understand
That our spirits dwell, deep inside every grain of sand, in this land
Every valley and every hill,
All endangered species we try to kill
It's they who make this island unique
For them my poem will always speak

CHORUS

I cried for this land, when I heard the old Piton plan
Cable cars to creep, from peek to peek
T'was 1992, I just couldn't believe what I heard was true
Our precious peaks for tourist to play hide and seek.
So I called the PM John, I was feeling young and strong
And told him that the Plan was wrong
He heard my Nobel voice, He had no other choice
And the Piton Plan was shut down
Again I cried, 2017 when the man decide
Maria Island gone, for tourist just to have their fun
I was horrified, that is why, I died

Verse 2

Every word I wrote, was Saint Lucia I did promote
Making us the popular destination of which we boast
All around the world, Saint Lucia's story is told
Through my books and poetry, our reputation is gold
But then again, back home I got no respect
My little house Chaussee road now they want to wreck, I object

A place the population should see
Expertly built in memory of me
It's like there's no Nationals we can trust
Cause the tools you see don't belong to us

CHORUS

I cried for this land, when I heard of the Dolphin Plan
These mammals should be, free at sea
I knew before you, I just couldn't believe what I heard was true
Dolphins in a cage to perform on a Tourist Stage
So you must call the PM Man, and tell Him that his plan
Is absolutely profane.
And if you do it with one voice, he will have no other choice
But to send the Plan down the drain
But again I cried, 2017 when the Man decide
Pigeon Island gone, for Dolphins just to prance around
I was horrified, that is why, I died.

The song is a tribute to Sir Derek Walcott, Saint Lucia's Nobel Laureate for literature in 1992 and speaks most passionately about his concern regarding some touristic developments and their likely negative environmental impact. He is internationally respected as a Literary Giant and for capturing the Essence of Saint Lucia and the Caribbean. Sir Derek Walcott passed away on 17th March, 2017 at the age of 87 years.

PEP Monarch Titles:

1987 "Unborn Child" & "Learn From Them"
1988 "En Bas Gorge La" & "Vagrant"
1992 "Bab Camawad" & "Rags to Riches"
1994 "Calypso Farewell" & "Alien"
1995 "The Will" & "Crime Wave"
2002 "Escape to Death" & "Last Days"
2009 "Taking a Chance" & "Get Off"
2017 "Why I Died" & "Fraid De Doctor"

I ran into Invader *(Ignatius Tisin)* right after the 2017 season. It was obvious that he had a disastrous season. He was disappointed at how negative the competition had become behind the scenes and the disrespect shown him by calypso authorities, some new kids on the block and even from some of the fans. It was as though they wanted to wish him away.

"Maybe you needed to reinvent yourself," I suggested. "Try new things: a new writing team; anything that would appear different; even removing the mask and instead of sitting awaiting invitations to appear at shows, you needed to organize some of your own shows in Castries, Vieux Fort, Soufriere and in some of the rural communities as you have done in the past."

There's no doubt that Invaders passion was gone and he was in a very dark place, undoubtedly reasons for withdrawing from the competition. My hope is that Invader bounces back, for calypso would not be the same without him. **Fast Forward** And bounce back he's done with the winning of the First Ever Kweyol Calypso Competition, one of the activities planned in October as part of Kweyol Heritage Month.

We all love the old Invader and how can we ever forget "Stay in your section" which won him the monarchy in 2010 or the 2007 classic, "My Eyeballs Hurting Me." An excerpt follows.

My Eyeballs hurting me

Well I came from Cuba
From a successful eye operation
Got back home just in time
For de General Election
All my friends were happy
Supporting de SLP
You would swear we done win
De Election already
Was billboards all over de country
Every weekend a rally
Even a Labour party cd

> *But dat night when election results started coming*
> *Man my tears I could not contain*
> *I cried so much that my balls started hurting again.....*
> *When I see in Central how dey lick down Dr. Vaughan*
> *My eyeballs hurting me*
> *My eyeballs hurting me*
> *Then I see how Mondesir decalay*
> *Cyprian*
> *My eyeballs hurting me*
> *Yes my eyeballs hurting me*
> *You see it proves, that you people you are de boss*
> *You are the ones who determine the course*
> *That is why my party lost*
> *Because contact with de masses you should maintain*
> *If votes you want to ascertain*
> *I cry so much dat my balls hurting again*
> *My eyeballs hurting me*
> *My eyeballs hurting me*

Invader has captured the crown in 1985, 1986, 1993, 2010.

Calypsonians have generally been able to reflect the mood of the people in the country and here's a song that makes an appeal to the politician, from his 2008 Calypso album "Suzette" with which he captured the crown that same year. The track is haunting and lilting as only Herb Black can deliver...

See About Them

> *Honesty they say is the best policy*
> *And we lack too much of it politically*
> *We all know that success does not come with ease no sir*
> *So come out an tell people de ting like it is*
> *For is dem who campaign*
> *Who stood to defend your name*
> *And vote you again, vote you again*
> *Yes, they still will be there*

For the next election year
Holding your emblem, so see about dem please politicians...

I sought Nahum Jn Baptiste, one of the most revered and successful composers, about his interest in the artform. "I became involved in 1989 when I was approached by the Ashanti (Herman Hippolyte) who asked me to write for him because his songwriter (Trevor "Jah T" Anthony) was not working with him that year. Herman and I are childhood friends and he knew of my love for calypso and music. I had read an interesting article on the growing population in the Voice newspaper, and used the facts from the article to compose my first calypso 'St. Lucia Growing Population', which turned out to be an instant hit and won the first calypso monarch for Ashanti in 1990. Since then he has won the crown with my compositions in 1991 and 1998, made the calypso finals and/or placed in the top four regularly."

Lucia Growin' Population (Ashanti, 1990)

Verse 1

Everybody cryin'
To control de growing population
From de family planning
To de teachers and calypsonian
And de minister givin' orders
To stop de baby factory
Every year de budget lectures
High population brings poverty
But despite all a dem problems
Lucia sexin' like she eh care
So she getting boom
With 4000 babies each year
And de population growin' rapid
By 3% I am told
Right now we in de lead
With de fastest rate in de world

So Lucia now lookin' for ways
To stop makin' all dem children
You know one dem days
She might even legalize abortion

Chorus

So Lucia now
In a critical situation
She doh know how
To control growing population
Like she eh care
She wild at carnival and fete
So every year
Is 4000 babies she get
While dey makin' big ro ro
Arguin' bout ting like casino
Lucia gettin' low low low
While she population grow grow grow

Shanti Tell Dem

Verse 1

While I sat
There to chat
With this old man de other day
He was born
Just around
1931 that de say
He tell me parents
Used to control deh children
Friends and neighbours even used to help dem
And de children were taught to respect deh elders
Fathers were around as de head of household
To keep de children under deh control
But then de war came and things changed altogether
He say that was when
A lot of children
Grew up without deh father
Female destitutes
Became prostitutes
From bread-winning pressure

Chorus

By then indiscipline start to progress
Morals start to regress
Children became lawless
Teenage pregnancy crime and drug abuse overgrow
Shanti tell dem in a kaiso (yes man)
Shanti tell dem so
Shanti make dem plan tomorrow
Shanti make dem wise
Shanti make dem open deh eyes

Verse 2

This old sage

Grey with age
Really started to make good sense
So I sat
There to chat
Just to get his experience
He tell me parents
Required a letter
From de man interested in their daughter
And he had to state, what was his intention
It was not rare for a girl at 19
To be without child or even a virgin
But by 1960 it was a different generation
Children made children
With deceitful men
Who ran away from deh role
Scanty dress fashion
Lit lustful passion
Dey no longer had self-control

Verse 3

To my mind
He was kind
This old man was gentle and wise
So I sat
There to chat
Just for him to open my eyes
He tell me parents
And teachers together
Scolded and rebuked
To stop bad behaviour
And dey never spared de rod to spoil de child
Civil servants teachers and policemen
Served as role models in my generation
But come de eighties de society had gone wild
Delinquent rascals

Juvenile vandals
Destroyed lives and property
Crooked officers
Took bribery dollars
From barons flaunting drugs money

Verse 4

Every word
That I heard
From this old man inspired me
So I sat
There to chat
To get lyrics for this melody
He tell me parents
Lived to teach deh children
Truthfulness respect and obedience
And de church used to teach parents morality
Excuse me please, thank you and I'm sorry
Were de norms used in my society
But by 1990 it was moral catastrophe
Sinful ministers
With double standards
No longer did what dey preach
Indecent language
Was common usage
Social order was out of reach

"We (Ashanti and I) were delighted when approached by Dave Samuels to participate in "The King, The Dread and The Buffalo" album project as it offered the first opportunity to document our work for posterity and future use. This is very important to me because it represents the first of the few quality studio recordings of my compositions. I remain thankful to Dave for this initiative, which he supported with his own time, expertise and money and increased access to our local calypsoes by other lovers of calypso music, including Saint Lucians in the diaspora", Naham recalled.

Then in 1996, he continued, "Menell (Menell Delice) asked me to write for her the following year because she wanted to make it to the finals. I discussed the new prospect with my friend and fellow songwriter Zepherin "Face" Calixte, who offered a brilliant idea in "Pass it on" for a first song, which we both worked on, but we needed a second song. What should I write about? The UWP had just won the elections in December, 2006, under the leadership of Sir John Compton, but the old fox/master strategist had fallen ill and his party had split into factions. I envisioned him on his sick bed witnessing what he had worked so hard to regain, being threatened by a bunch of greedy parasites, but he will not suffer this to happen if he is ill (and even after death) so I wrote "Still Holding On", which is arguably my biggest hit to date. Menell won the competition for the first time that year. After Sir John passed, I was approached by the Government to rework the lyrics to reflect his passing and I named the new version "Moving On".

Movin' On (Menell, 2007)

I love this country with all of my heart
Couldn't just sit and watch men rip her apart
That's why I made her independent
Gave my life postpone retirement
Though I knew I was not well from de start
But I had this last vision in my head
Wanted to share it before I lay dead
But this wish I did not fulfil
For it was not de Master's will
He summoned so I go to where he has prepared

Chorus

I was holding on
To de power you gave to me, Lucy
Till me last breath gone
I fought for my sweet St. Lucy
Did not let no one
Come and plunder this my country

Ah was holdin' on
Till Master was ready for me
So now Ah gone
To de after life
Ah movin' on
To Paradise
Ah movin' on
To the great beyond
Ah movin' on
To Glory Land
Till Judgment day come
Compy now movin' on
My memory lives on
Compy now movin' on
My work here is done
Compy now movin' on

Finally, Nahum reviews the 2017 calypso season;

"Judging needs to be reviewed," says Nahum, "as it's currently open to human judgment and bias. The idea of having different judges for the various stages of the competition is good, but the judges for each stage need to be randomly selected in advance so that it is known who they are and what stage they are judging and the method of removing the highest and lowest scores from a miniscule sample of 7 judges and then add the residual scores is ineffective in removing bias, when two or more judges are scoring particular calypsonians/songs markedly higher or lower. This method of avoiding bias is only effective for larger samples. In addition, scores ought to be collected after each song has been performed (preferably by a contracted auditor), quality checked, and immediately entered into an electronic database and made available within 45 minutes after the last performance" Nahum continues, "SCORES MUST NOT BE DISCUSSED OR CHANGED AT ANY TIME OF THE COMPETITION. Moreover, the judging panel should be equally representative for each criterion; Lyrics, Music, Performance and must have dedicated competence in judging the criterion they represent," advises Nahum

We end this Chapter with an excerpt from Lord Jackson (Mark Phillips) Calypso King 1980 and his 2007 "The Power of Calypso". written and composed by the Mighty Pelay.

> *Calypso Calypso a magnetic force*
> *Which captivate both de young an old among us*
> *A story teller, a great amuser*
> *And it has rhythm to set your body on fire*
> *With its double meaning*
> *It keeps you guessing*
> *As though it's a super novel you reading*
> *And within these qualities*
> *The power of Calypso emerges*
> *When with one song you can*
> *Truly enlighten de whole nation*
> *That is de power, de power of Calypso*
> *When someone you could criticize*
> *And this they cyar realize*
> *That is de power, de power of Calypso*
> *When you see a man at mid age*
> *Still eager to get on stage*
> *And my body say its time to go*
> *That is de power of Calypso*
> *That is de power of Calypso.*

Let us all as Saint Lucians at home and in the Diaspora, pay tribute to all former monarchs not highlighted in this story as well as the many calypsonians, writers, composers, and musicians who've given of their best to the artform, including all those who've passed over the years. We remember you.

CHAPTER 10

GEORGE ODLUM LIVES

"George Odlum took to the public platform in late 1969, at the highest point of UWP popularity. No political opportunist would do this. (Peter Josie MP Castries East 1978)

I don't recall how exactly I connected with George, but it wasn't any secret that most of my peers and I were captivated by his oratory brilliance and hands on mobilizational ability, and so when the SLP captured 7 seats to UWP's 10, the consensus was that the party would form the Government the next time around in 1979. Martinus Francois in his book "Hero" recounts the vote count that night this way. "It was the first time that Saint Lucia had been divided into 17 constituencies; and the first time that electors were able to vote at 18 years. Previously it had been 21 years; but perhaps, the most historic consequence of that night was the fatal stopping of George Odlum by 42 votes. Mrs. Heraldine Rock had beaten Odlum" 1063 to 1021 votes.

George Odlum was born on June 24th, 1934. His Father, Staffy, was a popular Castries barber and a man of honesty, integrity and high moral values. "I was part of a very big, gregarious and warm family and to handle a family of 11 on a measly income, took a masterstroke of economics for which my mom, Venice, gets all the credit". George was an outstanding student and talented footballer during his years at St Mary's College where he also taught for a short time. He attended both Bristol and Oxford Universities and did a first degree in Politics, Economics and Literature, becoming the first black to captain the university debating team and at Oxford, he read "Modern Greats at Magdaline College. In 1964 he took up the appointment as an economist with the Commonwealth Secretariat in London and later joined the West Indies Associated States Secretariat in Saint Lucia, and became one of the main voices of the Saint Lucia Forum - a pressure group which sought to educate the masses about the negative aspects of colonialism and the emergence of 'A New Saint Lucian/ Caribbean political thinking". It was therefore no surprise when he went into politics and ran for a seat in the 1974 General Election.

The events between then and 1982 were very disruptive and intense, especially in the Castries basin, with the SLP being victorious at the 1979 poll. Most young people swung to Labour during that era. I carried the Star symbol on the front and back windscreens of my silver Honda Accord Hatchback in the very heart of Flambeau country-Micoud. I visited the Canai family regularly and it still fascinates me up to this day that no one ever attempted to damage my vehicle in any way, which speaks volumes to the peaceful and loving nature of Micoudians." DS was a friend even though they may have disapproved of his politics". Of course we witnessed the eventual demise of the SLP three years later, a period which has already been documented by Rick Wayne and Peter Josie in their respective publications.

Nurse Muscette Canai was one of George's elder sisters and the affable and generous matriarch of the Canai clan and their Micoud home was in a sense my home away from home; Those heated Sunday afternoon political arguments at Uncle Jeff's Bar with Alvin, Allison, Chubs, Laurencia, Norman, Willard etc., are forever etched in my memory, so in a sense George saw me as *"Jean Kaye"* and even after he was crushed by the outcome of the 1982 General Election, we always kept in touch. I visited him often and dined at his Odin's Restaurant and bar at the waters edge in Marigot Bay during the late 80's and early 90's and after his fallout with the Kenny Anthony administration. We had morning coffee often during visits to "Valhalla" at Marigot. He was always supportive, offering advice on business, Arts and Culture and sharing views on English Literature and of course Politics.

I'd also visit the Odlum family home on St. Louis Street whenever I needed to get any information about what was happening, as back then things were usually politically charged and exciting. George was often there with some of his siblings, particularly Jon, and a number of supporters who would be milling around just to converse, or simply wanted to get an embrace from the brother. At other times he'd be in the Crusader building across the street which also housed the Bitter End Bar on the top floor where many of his supporters and some intellectuals would meet to discuss the issues of the week. The Crusader newspaper section was separated by a partition on the same floor. It was a weekly publication which hit the newsstands on Saturday mornings, but sometimes I was lucky to get my copy late Fridays from Buffalo, who for years had assisted his Uncle George to get the paper out in time for the next day. I can still hear the Clack Clack Clack of the running press in my head. George wrote with such depth and titillated your thinking in a manner not many others could. His biting and thought provoking editorials, the *Quick Quack* and *Cocky and Stocky* Columns were a "Must Read" and we are all the poorer for the void his passing has created, not only politically but journalistically.

Sometimes I wondered whether George understood what "House to House" campaigning was all about, that one usually had to "Meet and Greet" and "Touch Flesh" or simply "Hang Out" with the constituents on a regular basis. It was not here today and bye until next month, which I believe led to his many failures at the polls, coupled with the regularity in which he was demonized by his opponents and most sections of the press.

Love or hate him, many of us considered George a National Leader, though we had some doubt as to his electability. He was extremely uncomfortable asking or begging people to vote for him. It just wasn't part of his makeup. Ah! But a podium was his altar and he must have thought "the seat could be won" and that all he had to do was to open his mouth, speak, and perform, and that theatrical pedigree that was so inherently him, was nothing short of breathtaking. Sadly though, the only times he was victorious were during the national landslides towards Labour in 1979 and 1997.

I remember once writing a cheque to purchase a lawn mower for a Bexon community youth group, so as to assist his outreach to the youth in the Castries South East Constituency and advised him that quite apart from being at the formal presentation of the machine, he needed to step up his game plan and demonstrate that he was there with them, the way I coined it? "You need to be like another GEORGE!! MALLET! (*Castries Central MP, 1958 – 1996. Never lost an election*) Go to the wakes, the funerals, the christenings and all other social events including Sunday Mass, and regular visits to as many households as possible". He merely shrugged me off, shook his head and said, "So you want me to be a Mallet huh?" Laughed, nodded and that was it. I said no more on that issue.

Then in 1993, there was the offer by Prime Minister Compton to Odlum, to become the islands UN Ambassador. Says the PM "That a man of such immense talent and ability should not be wasting his time in Saint Lucia and so he'd given him the opportunity to put his skills to use for the benefit of all in the nation", but I'd already been aware of the offer, as George had confided in me, as I assumed he would have with family and close friends. "What do you think, Brother Dave?"; and I recall telling him how thrilled and happy I was for him, but I had wondered if it wasn't a strategic move by Compton to get him out of the way and he confirmed that he'd thought about that as well, but I countered "All things aside George, go for it!", and he did for a period of two years.

Then the surprise resignation from his post at the UN came in 1996. He returned to challenge Dr. Vaughan Lewis for the George Mallet vacated Castries Central seat (Mallet was appointed Governor General). Compton had controversially selected Lewis to succeed him as PM as he was retiring, a full year before constitutionally due elections. I recall my mother calling me at work during the Castries Central By-Election campaign and announcing excitedly, "Dave! You'd never guess who came to see me today and asked me to support him in the upcoming election?", I said to her, "Who?" and she replied, "Odlum"!

Some five years later in 2001, George teamed up with UWP leader Dr. Morella Joseph and Compton to form the ALLIANCE which was short-lived, mainly due to the uncertainty as to who would lead it, as well as their ideological differences, but he never sought my opinion about that until after the experiment had failed.

On September 11, 2001, I was at Valhalla with George, who was by then a shade of his old self combating pancreatic cancer. Lindsay, a younger brother, and I were having a conversation in the living room. The television was on but the volume was on mute. It was George who called out to us a little distance from his room to inform us of the events taking place that morning in the United States, when terrorists drove two commercial airlines into the Twin Towers of the World Trade Center, as well as the other aircrafts that were deliberately crashed by other terrorists a short while later. More than 3000 people perished that morning. Certainly a day never to be forgotten and yet another reason why George will always be remembered for I was at Valhalla that Tuesday, September 11, Yes! I was there! I miss George! I miss the passion and political education he brought to the masses. There was usually a "Hush" when he spoke and his ability to weave into **Kweyol** from English and back to **lang mama nou** was phenomenal. There is no one from any political party today who has been able to mesmerize and impact a crowd like George; No one even comes close!

One evening just a few months before he passed, I was driving to the city from the Morne and when I got to the stop just before the bridge, at the traffic lights adjacent to Duboulay's Bottling, my car stalled, so I got out and motioned to the motorist behind me that I had stalled. It was George. He drove ahead and then returned with two guys who helped push my car to a clearing near the Vieux Fort bus stand. He then waited for me while I placed a call to a mechanic friend and then shortly after took me to my destination point some miles away, promising to return to pick me up if I needed him to. That was the person who always showed concern for others and whom Dr. Ralph Gonsalves, St. Vincent and the Grenadines Prime minister described as "A giant of a man!"

Someone once referred to George as the great satan and a petty thief. Those words cannot be further from the truth. George was like a big teddy bear and so respectful of everyone. Even when he thought that you didn't support him politically, he was engaging and approachable which is a far cry from most of our politicians today, and so I've selected some of his comments and edited speeches, which I hope will give a better understanding, if not a different perspective, against the backdrop of all the negativity and controversy that had dogged him throughout his political career.

BAD BOY GEORGE

I agree that I've been labelled as the Bad guy continually. I understand that so well, and I have the inner strength of knowing that the perception is wrong. I know that the media has done a particularly devastating job on me, not as much the electronic media as the print media; denigration of character, projecting me as a Communist now and as a passport donor another time and the accumulation of these things in the consciousness of the people create a fear. I know that I am not all these things and that's why I can stand up against the whole train and defend my actions and my views all the time.

WHAT ACCOMPLISHMENTS?

Some people see my contribution in terms of not having accomplished things, in terms of positions held, but I don't see it like that at all. I see my job as lifting the quality of life of the community, educating as much as I can, and giving as much as I got. I always thought that my education was the property of the community and not of my own, I always feel that anything I have is something I have as a result of the community and it must be shared with the community.

OBSTACLES TO NATIONAL GROWTH

There are a number of built in obstacles which impede the evolution and growth of our society. The first of these is the attitude of our people which constitutes a bottleneck to development. We have failed to excite and energize our people to take into their hands the responsibility of being the engine for growth in our society. Our government must "Prime the Pump", but our people must also respond creatively and productively to these incentives. If we fail to motivate our people to produce efficiently, then we will fall out of the global race for development. This is indeed a serious situation, and the division of our society, the tribalised position of our party supporters and the absence of the overriding national pride, will prevent us from making any progress as a nation. The division in our society is indeed a serious obstacle to development.

The media feels it has a professional responsibility to hold the mirror up to the level of hostility and discontent which is prevalent in our society. We must devise a system which will bring our people together as a united force, which will increase the efficiency, productivity and competitiveness of our country. It is a bold step but we must seize the time. Otherwise the rapid pace of global events will overwhelm us as the culture of hate and division is gaining strength. The society is getting fiercely polarized again and it is incumbent upon us to move positively to find a fresh formula for healing this nation. Our leaders must put their heads together with the leaders of the church and the leaders of the community to explore the possibility of uniting our people and our country and to enable us to chart a better way of life for our people, that is, a way of life rooted less in personal interest and more in nation building.

FIGHTING THE SYSTEM

I've been trying to explain to the Chambers of Commerce in the area and to the people who are more fortunate or privileged in the society that in order to enjoy their wealth, their affluence, their greater luxury or their greater leisure, they must ensure that the masses of the people are satisfied and enjoy their basic needs. You cannot enjoy affluence when you're surrounded by indigence and want. You cannot sleep at nights, if the people who work for you are dissatisfied and restless, so if you want to sleep at nights, you must concern yourself with the lot of the ordinary man. This is a simple doctrine; and as simple as it is, a lot of people cannot understand that simple point. As simple as it is, the ordinary man can understand it more than the man at one removed in the higher income bracket. That is why all around us we see opportunism - men falling prey to money, position and bribes. This is part of the system that we are fighting and when we are sucked in by this we are no more. The new breed of men must rise above the level of opportunism. They must dedicate themselves with sacrifice and firm commitment to the struggle of the people at large.

EN WAJAY FOR PRIME MINISTER?

I am happily not pre-occupied with conventional notions of success and failure. I will have to concede that I failed to achieve certain things, although not being Prime Minister of Saint Lucia is not one of them. My objectives were not that limited. My objective is to awaken and broaden the consciousness of the people of Saint Lucia; to educate them politically and culturally and to inculcate a sense of values in our people. In the course of the elections of 1974, 1979 and 1982, the zeal and passion with which I conducted my campaigns left my enemies, or shall we say political rivals, with no other conclusion but that I was *enwajay* for prime minister. They fondly felt that the motive force behind all my political activity was a consuming desire to be Prime Minister. Nothing is further from the truth. I always saw my participation in government as part of a sacrifice which I had to make to fulfill a deep-seated desire to serve my people. Such service was not restricted to government. I saw my contributions as part of a grassroots, workers' thrust, since the development strategy would turn on the enlightenment and promotion of the common man.

20/20 Vision:

When you are confronted with mortality, you get a rather clearer vision of things. You notice all the time you've spent in politics and realize that political division has not done the people of the country much good. We have to try a new way, a way to bind the people and make them born again, but it must be people who cannot be accused of material self interest.

When you have a narrow leadership that is only concerned with staying in power for the next election or canvassing a vote here and there, sometimes that generates negative reactions within the community. The people have to have the confidence that politicians in power are not conning them, while putting money in their pockets. Politicians need a new credibility and they need to utilize the important spiritual leaders of our society. If God gave me the strength to continue any kind of work, I would be in a completely new dimension.

In my life, I have put my people and my country above my family and above friends who were close to me. My vision and mission involved the broad mass of people whom we have to push forward for the betterment of Saint Lucia. The people should feel that those working for them are working strongly in their interest. They should not feel that they have a Government with personal axes to grind and that they are not getting greedy and more acquisitive. Also the media should not be used just to push the interest of the Government, but to explore the creative possibilities of the community. To move forward Government must form an alliance with all the main spiritual leaders in the country, take all of them and bring them together and let them pull this community together, hand in hand with the political directorate. That's where the spirituality comes in-and that's the way to go now.

ZONE OF PEACE

Today in the Caribbean, it is important that our foreign ministers make a projection for peace. We must try to declare the Caribbean area as a zone of peace. We must be careful that the Caribbean territories are not used as pawns in bringing about a division in the Caribbean itself. We must not be party to any isolation of any territories, or any interference in the domestic affairs of any individual Caribbean territory. We must respect the sovereign right of these territories at all times and I cannot emphasize strongly enough, the need to be wary at the fact that people or nations or international communities pursuing their own personal interest, would not be aversed to dividing the Caribbean in the process.

AN INTIMATE PORTRAIT OF NEVILLE CENAC (CHANDELL MOL)

Many a Labour supporter has rushed to the Castries market steps to listen to the somewhat unique performance of young Neville Cenac. Flouting his flamboyance with a white towel turban or an outsize red cravat, the willowy Cenac can sting with waspish accuracy. He can cajole or flatter with a Creole turn of phrase that would warm the cockles of our grandmother's heart. This art of vivid bilingual speech making springs not from any natural cunning of the Cenac tongue. It springs from a studied grace, a carefully organized mind...Neville Cenac is almost completely identified with the Labour movement during the past decade. He kept the light of the Labour star flickering when the fortunes of the party was at its lowest ebb. He charmed the Labour followers and kept their hopes alive with his peculiar blend of comedy and high seriousness.

Sir Emmanuel Neville Cenac became Saint Lucia's sixth Governor General in January, 2018.

STATE POWER

Most political parties sport a political agenda with one single item-The acquisition of State power. They are reckless about the most Important items which should pack a political agenda.

* Has the party got the leadership capability to promote, guide and develop the country?
* Has the party attracted sound, competent and committed persons to rise to the challenges of modern Government?
* Has the party a body of principles and a programme for stabilizing and rescuing the country?

The challenges of Government today surpasses the superficiality of getting into office: It is concerned more with the retention of state power through the implementation of fundamental policies and plans. It is the "intangibles" which hold the key to political survival. One such intangible is CORRUPTION.

One of the characteristic features of REVOLVING DOOR POLITICS is that the incoming Party interprets state power as a mandate to take over all the benefits, all the excesses, all the perks and all the corruption which the outgoing regime indulged in! "It is our TURN!". It was the failure of the Labour leadership to deal firmly and decisively with these matters which introduced the urgency to challenge the leadership. An insecure leadership takes refuge in granting immunity to wrong-doers. An insecure leadership never punishes corruption and illegality in the fond hope that this leniency will buy support and not alienate wrong-doers. Any reliance on corruption breeds deeper corruption. The failure to punish wrong-doing is one of the most subversive elements in Saint Lucian society today. A number of Ministers of Government have invested their money and their time to becoming Ministers solely with a view to being in the red-meat of corrupt practices. The question of SERVICE never arose!

TIM HECTOR EULOGIZED.

Dear Brother and Comrade-in-arms, I have no need to praise you, since our friendship and our lives together have been a mutual hosanna of praise, acceptance and affirmation of the principles we stood for and the values we espoused. We did this in the face of tremendous odds and spirited opposition from a society whose philistinism has become a by-word.

Ironically, you lived and died in the pursuit of a body of values, which were meant to elevate a Caribbean society and forge a creative and dynamic people out of the detritus which history has bequeathed on us. You fought to explain that history and to analyze it in the interest of the ordinary man and woman, but the forces of reaction were strongly arrayed against you.

As you lie there motionless and still in your fine resplendent mahogany casket, I cannot help but feel a sense of mockery that the same society which vilified and ridiculed you when your strident voice embarrassed them with your message and your clarion calls, is the same society that will embrace and elevate you now that your mighty heart is lying still. Where is the logic in this my brother? Today, as I contemplate your mortality, I cannot suppress the insistent feeling that the people of Antigua and to a lesser extent the Caribbean, have thrown away a pearl richer than all their tribe. This is a serious accusation to make against a society that has turned out in large numbers to pay homage to this dead Viking. But many of you stood by over the years and witnessed the victimization and demoralization of Tim Hector and never lifted a finger to prevent it. Were you there when they crucified Tim Hector? Were you there? Were you there when they nailed him to the cross? Were you there when they dragged him through the courts? Were you there? Were you there when they dumped him to the prison for his views? Were you there when they burned his printing press? Were you there?....But my dear Brother, do not be too complacent in your casket, do not go gently into the dark night. Rage! Rage! Rage against the passing of the light. Rage into the consciousness of the young, so that they too will be moved to keep the fire burning and fan the flame for humanity. See you in Valhalla!

The following is a statement by Mr. Jerry E. M. George, Co-ordinator George Odlum Remembrance Celebration Committee - January 26, 2018

George Odlum is an enigmatic and imposing figure in Saint Lucia's history. The story of his contribution to national life is unfolding and what that story is depends on who you ask. Today, even years after his death, Odlum's name is resurrected whenever the nation seems at the crossroads, as the voice of righteous indignation that needs to be heard, not only for an analysis of the issues confronting the ordinary man but also for articulating them with eloquence and passion – whether in Kweyol or in English.

The George Odlum Remembrance Celebration Committee was formed to celebrate the life and contributions of George Odlum to national and international development, not only just as a politician – though there is always the temptation to pigeon hole him in only in this sphere - but also as a whole multisided individual, with sterling contributions in sports, the arts/culture, in journalism, a family man and a man who had an unquestionable love for his country. Through our annual Memorial Lecture, we provide an opportunity to explore how his contributions have raised the consciousness of generations and how he sought to make a difference in the lives of all who heard his messages whether at the Castries Market steps, in his Crusader newspaper, in the Saint Lucia Parliament or as an accessible giant in one-on-one conversations.

As the Chairperson of the Committee, I know that our effort with the commemorative lecture series is bearing some fruit based on the increasing numbers that attend each year. And I know that the Committee is committed to bringing to the public's attention those who can speak on all aspects of his life and contributions. We are aware that the history of Saint Lucia in which Odlum is featured cannot be one-sided. We aim to delve deep into all sides to arrive to the truth about the whole person who is George Odlum, a man who helped in the shaping of a people to face their destiny with confidence and dignity.

George Odlum's life transcends all efforts to demonize him as the political radical by those who believe his name cannot, on one hand be mentioned in the same breath as Sir John Compton, whom Odlum once described as "the darling boy of the establishment"; and whom the establishment viewed always with suspicion and unease for his role in awakening the political consciousness of the masses at a time in the nation's political history when most needed. On the other hand, Odlum is seen as a charming statesman with an imposing presence on the international stage who can expound on any topic but always making the perspectives of small island states his priority. Of course, both sides have their merits, but where the problem arises is when one side is ignored in favour or ignoring of the other.

Jerry E. M. George

Dame Pearlette Louisy

Sir John Compton

Conversations

Dr. Kenny D. Anthony

Hon. Allen Chastanet

CHAPTER 11

A CONVERSATION WITH DAME PEARLETTE LOUISY GOVERNOR GENERAL OF SAINT LUCIA - (1997 – 2017)

"ENDEARING"

Dame Pearlette Louisy is the first female Governor General of Saint Lucia and the longest serving Governor General in the history of the 52-nation Commonwealth.

We sat down to do the interview for this publication at Government House just a few weeks before she demitted office, on December 31, 2017.

Born in the quaint fishing village of Laborie, she became the principal of the Sir Arthur Lewis Community College (SALCC) and can boast of a distinctive career in academia.

Among other academic achievements, she ha an MA degree in Linguistics from the University of Laval in Quebec, Canada, and a Doctor of Philosophy degree in Education from the University of Bristol, England and in 1999, while being Saint Lucia's Head of State, an honorary degree of Doctor of Laws (LLD) from that institution and an honorary degree of Doctor of Laws from the University of the West Indies (LLB)

Dame Pearlette has also had two knighthoods bestowed on her; the Most Venerable Order of Saint John (UK) and the Equestrian Order of Saint Gregory the Great (Vatican). She's also the recipient of Saint Lucia's highest honour, the Grand Cross of Saint Lucia. Her Excellency has served six administrations since 1997.

The Traditional Guidance Notes issued to Governors-General, discouraged holders of the Office from granting interviews to the press or to representatives of commercial organisations or magazines. This was meant to safeguard them from making public comments that might conflict or give the appearance of conflicting with their constitutional role. However, in this new information age where the Governor-General's appearances at both public and private events are so instantaneously available, these precautions no longer seem so relevant. Moreover, there is a timely move on the part of Saint Lucians to document our history and to tell our stories so that these can be understood by contemporaries and transmitted to be emulated or avoided. This is Dame Pearlette's story as she lived it during the two decades she served as Governor General of Saint Lucia. ***This is her "VOICE".***

Q: Your Excellency, It's been 20 years since you've been Governor General of Saint Lucia. How best would you describe that journey?

A: Its been truly a learning experience. I've had some challenges, but I feel that perhaps I may have not done too badly, despite my early apprehension of accepting the position. I was still very much in my academic mood having recently returned from my doctoral studies, in an area in which I thought I would have made my professional career; the management of tertiary education, so to have been offered the position of Governor General of which I knew very little about, was quite a dramatic development. Admittedly, it wasn't a post that had been publicly discussed, so I was a bit apprehensive and thought long and hard over it. An opportunity to serve as Head of State is not to be scoffed at, so I accepted the offer.

The decision was made easier when I was told by then Prime Minister, Dr. Anthony, "to define the post as you see it", and so for the past twenty years I've been trying to articulate in my mind the mission of the Office, its relationship to Government: Legislative, Executive and the Judiciary arms, in kinship with the people of whom I am head. What kind of relationship that should exist between the Governor General and the people? It occurred to me that I couldn't be leading a nation if I'm far removed from them and their daily concerns about life. This is what has propelled me to take a different approach to things, become involved as much as possible with the citizenry, try to get them to accept that we are one community, all helping to develop our country.

So this is the mission of the Office of the Governor General which I came up with:

1. To provide leadership in the areas in which I have some kind of expertise.
2. To pursue the development of the economic, social and cultural life of the nation, and in this regard I've been involved in activities at different levels, quite apart from the constitutional ones, reaching out to the communities, the young, the old, and the in between. The inclusiveness that I've been trying to engender, hopefully has been successful to some degree, in showing people that this is what we are as a nation.

Q: Many people have been surprised that you've held on to the office for that long. Your predecessors would have served for about five years. Given your extremely flattering credentials in the education sphere, wouldn't you have considered moving to a position which may have helped shape the educational policy of the country?

A: Ah! But you'd have to belong to the group that does that. It's the political directorate who shapes policy so I would have had to enter the political arena and become a cabinet minister. I suppose one can do so through the Senate of course! If I had demitted the office earlier, I think I would have made a contribution at the regional level, at UWI perhaps, or there were offers from further afield-The University of Bristol in England with whom I have close ties, or I could have gone to UNESCO. But, to move on to a job at the regional and international level may have sent a wrong signal to the citizenry. Some would have got the wrong impression that I had abdicated my service to country in search of greener pastures so I decided to stay on and try to make a mark, you know, define the role I should play as Governor General.

Q: Would you share some of the highs and lows that you've experienced?

A: The Highs? The opportunities I was given to recognize the people of Saint Lucia. We did have the National Honors and the National Awards, but those were always very low keyed events and announced during Independence activities and that was it. Those were national awards and as such, needed to be visible and so I instituted the Investiture Ceremony at the National level. Also, in recognition of good service, my chairing of the Festival Nobel Laureate Committee, again to constantly place in the national consciousness, excellence, achievement and recognition. My involvement as Head of State and Opening of Parliament is a constitutional duty and responsibility, but I was given the opportunity to be more inclusive, to speak to the nation in a language that a lot of people would be more comfortable with and which was not previously done in a structured and more formal way, but always with the need to ensure public education and so I always take the opportunity to teach or to bring something to the attention of the public.

The Low points? My challenge to get persons to appreciate the Office of the Governor General, its role, what kind of courtesies to be afforded and extended to it, the lack of appreciation I dare say, from the legislative and the executive arm of Government as to the real function and nature of the Office of the Governor General. Too often people are dismissive of the Office as purely ceremonial.

DS: One hears this being debated all the time...

A: And I ask what does this mean? It's as if you're just brought out periodically and paraded around the streets so the fact that I've not been able to impress upon people the importance of this office is very troubling. The Office is an agent of Government that needs to be funded, the level of service that needs to be given and the fact that I have to struggle in getting assistance in maintaining the physical property. It's as though there wasn't any interest or enthusiasm in spending money on the Office of the Governor General.

Q: Do you think that all this stems from growing apathy and anti-monarchy sentiment? You represent Her Majesty the Queen and it may be that a constitutional change to a republic, with a President as a replacement for the Governor General, may be more acceptable to the nay sayers perhaps?

A: I don't really think so, unless the President is given executive powers. Unfortunately, many people do not see my office as contributing to the economic development of the country. People see development as largely economic but there is social and cultural development. So, it's really an understanding of what development is. Maybe a Head of State with executive powers would change people's concept of what a Governor General should be.

Q: The Kweyol language has been somewhat of a paradox. Without a doubt it has enhanced our oral cultural expression immeasurably, but while it continues to be spoken widely in the rural areas, there are many in urban and suburban Saint Lucia who still scoff at the use of it and would prefer if it wasn't used at all. Clearly, there is a lack of appreciation for its value. How can we get people to accept what is intrinsically us as a developing nation?

A: We are a Kweyol people and the language is just one aspect of our Kweyolness. Some people associate Kweyol with under development and its use is being blamed for some of the illiteracy and backwardness here, a feeling that it would be better for us to leave it behind where it belongs. Kweyol is part of the Saint Lucian experience. We have to learn that running away from who we are is never going to work and that we must get over the ambivalence we have towards the language and culture. Our people need to understand that this is us, this is our call, and that we have been socialized in that particular experience. Sometimes I listen to the debate about the teaching of Kweyol in schools and I feel that there needs to be a bit of openness to the whole idea of what somebody's native language means to a people.

There are two things: The use of Kweyol and the teaching of it. I'm sure that we can all agree that many things said in English, do not have the same impact as when expressed in Kweyol. I've been observing and studying some of the attitudes towards its use over the years and I think it's unfortunate that we've not reached further along the way. I hear some people ask, 'Where is Kweyol going to take us?', but we have to be practical. English is the internationally recognized language so we have to speak it, but we need to be grounded in our own.

Q: **Just as a follow up, What is your understanding about the use of Kweyol in Dominica for instance? Are they more accepting of their Kweyol than we are?**

A: We speak more Kweyol in Saint Lucia than Dominicans do on a daily basis. Somehow more English is spoken there. Even they acknowledge that we speak more Kweyol than they do. One of the models that I always refer to is the Seychelles, where Kweyol is the official language, next English and then French, but in the business of Government, Enterprise and Schools, you're taught in Kweyol and that has not affected the country's development. People think that if Kweyol is taught in schools, it will be to the total exclusion of English but that cannot be so. Kweyol should not make you any less able or capable. It's just about changing the mindset. Now, I might add, that this may have something to do with Haiti. Some people argue that the Haitian connection has not helped but it is the largest speaking Kweyol nation in this hemisphere and despite its political, economic, and social challenges and more recently the fairly consistent natural disasters, no one can doubt that they are a very talented and resilient people, achieving many great things all over the world. However, for some reason, we seldom hear of those exploits.

Q: You've served four Prime Ministers since assuming office in 1997. Dr Anthony, Sir John, Mr. King and now Mr. Chastanet. Give us some insight into what it has been like working with them?

A: The relationship with the Prime Ministers have been good, some a little less formal than others. Dr. Anthony, as you know, brought me in. He gave me the space and the opportunity to mold and shape the office, so having served with him the longest, there was more of a rapport. He visited regularly. If I had to raise any issues with the others, excluding Sir John of course, who wasn't in office for too long, it's that the constitution says that the Governor General should be kept fully abreast or updated about things that affect the country. Just a visit from time to time to inform me as to what is happening, would give me the opportunity to seek clarification. I hear things in the public domain and it would be useful to get some reaction from the Prime Minister.

I may have some ideas that need to be ventilated. For instance, you spoke about educational policy a while ago. I used to have wide ranging discussions with Dr. Anthony, but with PM King and now PM Chastanet, they seldom visit so I don't have the opportunity to seek clarification about myriad issues. It may very well be how they perceive the office, but you see, you really can't force them to come to you. However, it really makes for better governance if that were to occur on a fairly consistent basis. They've all been very cordial though, but as I've said, it's that rapport, that conversation, which is very much lacking.

Q: The nation seems to be polarized and that is to be expected during an election campaign, but once the election is over, the country and the people settle down. However this hasn't been the case of late. How does the glaring polarisation impact you as Head of State?

A: It is challenging, distressing and at times stressful because you do not and ought not to be in the middle of the controversies. In response, some people keep asking "Why is the Governor General so quiet or why isn't she speaking out?", but I cannot speak out against the policies of the Government. Apart from that, one really wants to pour some oil over those troubled waters, rather than inflame it by giving or even offering a hint as to my personal views.

Q: Now to the question of party colors and your attire at certain events. I recall seeing you at the swearing in ceremony of Sir John Compton's cabinet at the Prime Minister's official residence in 2006, in what appeared to be a lemon dress but which many saw as yellow, and at the Opening of the Parliament in 2017, in a fuchsia colored outfit which appeared to be red to many people. How much of a challenge is it to avoid anything that looks like a party color so as to appease supporters and indeed party officials of both camps?

A: In the beginning it got to me that people would react that way. Yes! I wore my "Chartreuse" lemon colored dress, then lately in my flamboyant "Fuchsia" dress with matching hat and it astounded me that even the politicians awaiting my reading of the throne speech in the House of Parliament were saying, "Why on earth is she wearing red for?" and "What statement is she trying to make?" So, what does it really matter? Those colors were there long before the establishment of both political parties. Red-signifies Christmas, Valentine, *La Rose* flower festival and a traffic light. Yellow-part of our national flag, a banana peel and most of our ripened fruit, also a traffic light color and the golden glow of an awesome Saint Lucian sunset.

Q: So! How do we begin to change that mindset?

A: Well! The people who put themselves up for office should be the ones to take the lead and get people to understand that this is really not what matters. Indeed you have the colors to differentiate the political parties during campaigns at election time which is understandable. I have to admit that I don't like to court disaster if it can be avoided, so it depends on where I'm going. If it's a national event, my wardrobe is full of blue outfits. I love color, bright colors. So we really need to rise above that. It has become ridiculous, really!

Q: Still about your attire, dresses, bags, hats with matching shoes. Who advises you?

A: Thanks to the Internet these days. I do have family in the UK and the US who would send me links to the various sites and I place my orders.

Q: Your hats are the focus of a great deal of debate with every fashion conscious woman, and some men I might add, all wondering, "What is she going to wear this time around?"

A: I hardly think about that, as those events are usually quite stressful and tiring. Opening of the Parliament, Independence etc. I know that they look forward to it so I really do make an effort. I also know that some people look to see if I'm wearing something that I've worn before. (laughs) Making an address like the throne speech for example, takes a lot of work, practice, practice, practice, voice inflection, intonation and moving into the back and forth from English to Kweyol is very hard work and it takes a lot of effort if you are to do it well and to deliver it well.

Q: You've endeared yourself to the populace. They find you humble, warm, down to earth, approachable, a role model and always so endearing. What advice would you like to offer to the people out there?

A: I'm tremendously flattered by those sentiments which are expressed in various ways. I say to people who say that I'm a role model, that I would be very happy if I saw the modeling. What I would like them to do is to model me. Now, I'm not super human but it takes effort. There are days when I don't want to go anywhere for three to five hours, but I've accepted to go, so this is what it is, so I'm going. I also want to say that in the workplace, whenever we move on, that we must all strive to leave our job better than we found it. It's my definition of good stewardship. Government House is going to be better when I leave than how I found it.

Q: **Your legacy? What would you like to be most remembered for?**

A: I would like to be remembered for what I've tried to do: my community outreach; to make an improvement towards national life and in the economic, social and cultural life of the country. "She came, she tried, she worked hard" and I would hope that a number of things I've started would not be discontinued after I've left...

Q: **Any advice for the people of Laborie, your home village, as well as the staff here at Government House?**

A: (Laughs) Laborie has honored me not just as Governor General, but even before as someone who's achieved much. Recently, a group of us have come together to determine what has made Laborie the special place that it is.

DS: **It's the level of community spirit among other things.**

A: Yes! The community spirit. The helping out and this is what I'd want them to continue. In my formative years that is what Laborie has always taught us. Staff? Its been a good team and I say to them always that we have to continue to mirror excellence in every sense of the word.

Q: **Life after being Governor General?**

A: I still do my writing of academic material published in some journals but mainly in Education, particularly Tertiary Education in small states and I will most probably continue with that. I may write about my tenure as Governor General but I would not want to finish with public life at this time. I would like to remain in the areas in which I have some expertise - Education and Culture. These are the areas in which I would really like to continue.

Q: Any comments about some of the activities planned to commemorate your 20th anniversary as Head of State?

A: About two years ago a group of about twelve people decided to form a Legacy committee to work towards some activities in honor of my 20th anniversary. It was really an initiative of Dr. Paris. At the end of the two weeks of activities, I told them that "You all will kill me!", because there were so many activities (A hearty laugh) The events all went very well and I am very appreciative of the support we got from the general public: The Ecumenical service, the renaming of the road in Laborie and the academic evening with Fr. Anthony. (Paba) I also want to say a big thank you to all for making it such a memorable month.

Q: Final thoughts?

A: It hasn't been the norm for Governors' General to grant interviews and it's been part of the protocol, but times have changed. This is the information age and I've discerned a sort of reticence and reluctance in Saint Lucia to document our history and I thought that this needs to change. Hence the reason why I've given interviews from time to time. Anything that documents our national life should be embraced. In spite of my ubiquitousness and our predilection for lateness, we should stop saying that the Governor General is always on time. We all should strive to be on time for everything, not just in attending an event, but doing things in a timely manner. The leisurely way we are prone to doing things in Saint Lucia needs to be revisited. Otherwise we are going to miss the boat.

..........Twenty 4 Twenty...........
20 Comments about Her Excellency

- A remarkable woman whom I had observed from very early, developing from an oyster into a Saint Lucian pearl. (ettc)
- She once said to me "No one will give you anything, especially as a woman. Earn your way and respect by developing you". I am so very proud of her and she remains my mentor and role model. Certainly, a woman beyond her time.
- My past SJC teacher: an educator, linguist, cultural activist, role model, Dame-Par Excellence. The youngest and first female Governor General has served with grace and distinction worthy of emulation in Saint Lucia and the Caribbean.
- She knows her work, is unpretentious and down to earth. I consider her the people's Governor General.
- Quite apart from the dignity and class with which she conducts herself, she has tried very hard to impart her love of reading and encourages the pursuit of educational advancement.
- What struck me the most about her is her fearlessness in telling the very Government that appointed her, that they were disrespecting her.
- Her performance as Governor General has been exceptional among those who have served in that position. She truly stands out!
- It is to the credit of Her Excellency that she has kept Government House and the grounds in such immaculate condition. It gives me such pride when I see visitors at the main entrance taking photographs with the grounds and the Great House as a backdrop.
- She has connected with the ordinary man in a way that her predecessors didn't and to a great degree couldn't.
- Her infusion of French Kweyol into Parliament and her championing of recognition for Saint Lucia's intellectual affluence through the Annual Nobel Laureate Week Celebration, are among the plethora of hallmarks of her illustrious tenure.
- Dame Pearlette is an exceptional Governor General. She's eloquent, charming, graceful, very approachable, always immaculately dressed-A phenomenal woman!

- A sterling, dignified performance. She is punctual at every event and carries out her duties with grace. Her use of Kweyol as part of the Throne Speech to Parliament, underscores her humility. She has not forgotten her roots-A true role model and extraordinary woman.

- She is a woman of pride, dignity and integrity. A woman worthy of admiration and emulation. With simplicity and humility she serves the nation, rendering outstanding leadership irrespective of the Government in office.

- Her Excellency continues to demonstrate her commitment to the growth and development of the nation's children and the well being of the elderly and less fortunate, through her participation in many different programs. May God richly bless her for her dedicated service.

- The dignity and stature she has personified makes one wonder whether Saint Lucia will, in the future, even consider having another male Governor General. She has most certainly shattered the proverbial "Glass Ceiling".

- Dame Pearlette rolls out a welcome red carpet at Government House to all Saint Lucians. Government House is accessible to *La Woz* groups, Service groups, Sports teams. *Tout moun*! This has added to the mystic of the Office as well as the person holding the office.

- One wonders if there couldn't be an "Open day" at Government House for visitors on a weekly or fortnightly basis, so they could enjoy the ambiance and the panoramic view of the city and beyond. This could provide some revenue towards the maintenance of such a wonderful property.

- She has become endeared to all for her wide brimmed hats and coordinated attire, yet has remained grounded as "just a girl from Laborie". Even in her official engagements, you will see her take time to mingle with ordinary folk. Never aloof, always accommodating.

- Dame Pearlette is kind, considerate, modest, unassuming and calm. Her quiet dignity, dedication to duty and pleasantness are worthy of emulating. Her Excellency always treats everyone with respect earning their admiration. Her character speaks volumes....

- Our Head of State has brought grace, class and professionalism to the office of Governor General. She is charismatic, a devout Catholic and has brought a ladies touch to a position that has been dominated by males only. Thank you your Excellency for making Saint Lucia proud and for your uncontroversial 20 years of service.

CHAPTER 12

A CONVERSATION WITH SIR JOHN COMPTON

"VISIONARY"

One of the high points of any broadcaster's career must surely be the encounters he has in the course of doing his job. I was fortunate over the years to have interviewed a host of personalities including local and regional celebrities, as well as Civil Society, Religious, Public Sector, Private Sector and Political Leaders. I consider some of my best interviews were with leaders in the political sphere especially those with Sir John George Melvin Compton, the man whose stamp is on Saint Lucia's development thrust, in the years both preceding and after independence. Sir John led Saint Lucia as Chief Minister, Premier and Prime Minister for 30 years across two different periods of constitutional advancement and presided over some of the most exciting times in Saint Lucia's development history. What is not often debated but is truly extraordinary, is Sir John's uninterrupted presence in the legislature. He first entered that chamber as an independent candidate for the then constituency of Micoud/Dennery in 1954, until the general election of 1997 as the MP for Micoud South, an unbroken stint of 43 years. He retired, then returned in 2006 to recapture the seat, to lead his party to victory once again until his passing in 2007, after a short illness.

The interview was broadcast over state-owned Radio Saint Lucia as part of Saint Lucia's 25th anniversary of Independence in 2004, and remains one of the most sought after interviews because of its historical content. The following are some of the highlights of the encounter.

Q: Sir, you are generally regarded as the father of Saint Lucia's independence. How do you react to such a title?

A: I accept it with all humility. It is something that goes down in history, no matter what happens, so I am part of Saint Lucia's history from now on. I am very humble about it but very proud.

Q: You took Saint Lucia to Independence from Associated Statehood. Were you comfortable with that decision against the backdrop that the Saint Lucia Labour Party wanted as a condition for Independence, a referendum, which you were obviously opposed to?

A: I didn't take the Labour Party's concerns in my calculation. My calculation was that Saint Lucia should move from colonialism. Independence (for Saint Lucia) alone was not my first choice. I worked very hard to see if we could have got the Associated States together; second the Windward Islands, and after we saw that there was no chance... Grenada had gone into Independence, then Dominica... there was no point just hanging around, so I decided that the best course for Saint Lucia was Independence alone. Just before Independence there was an election in 1974 and in the Throne Speech of that year I said, "Together if we can, alone if we must". There was no chance of the islands going together so we decided to go alone. The Labour Party's objection at the time was one of opportunism. Having lost the 1974 elections, they were trying to get another shot at the grand prize by saying we should have a referendum or elections before Independence, which had never happened in any one of the former colonies. It didn't happen in Jamaica, Trinidad and Tobago, Barbados, anywhere, so why should Saint Lucia be the exception? Because the Labour Party said so? Their objection was not part of my calculation. My calculation was the future of Saint Lucia.

DS: But the Labour Party seemed to have galvanized a great deal of support. Just prior to Independence there was a lot of political and social unrest in the country...

A: They didn't galvanize any support, but there was political and social unrest and if you look at the figures of the elections of that year, it was the result of pure terrorism. Most of the people abstained from voting because they were afraid...they were threatened.

Q: So was it calculated to keep your supporters at home?

A: Yes! yes! because everywhere we held meetings they were there. They used to truck people from one meeting to another. If we had two or three meetings, they would rent people to throw stones and intimidate. Of course, the decision had already been made. We had to go. We had to be independent and threatening people and throwing of stones did not in any way impede my progress for Independence.

Q: What do you remember most about the constitutional talks in London? What was the highlight for you?

A: What I remember most was the obstinacy of the Saint Lucia Labour Party, quibbling and wasting a lot of time and predicting all types of serious consequences if Saint Lucia became Independent.

Q: Were you intimidated by that?

A: Not at all, but at that time we had a British Government Representative here named Eric Le Tocq. He had just come from Botswana bordering on South Africa and he was convinced that black people could not rule themselves. He was a racist of note, and everything the Labour Party did, he magnified it and sent it to the Colonial Office, so he was the main ally of the Saint Lucia Labour Party in us not getting Independence at the time that we wanted it. Then we had another BGR, Stanley Arthur, who came to Saint Lucia and was staying at the Malabar Hotel. One night supporters of the Labour Party marched up to there and mashed up the place while he was there, because they were protesting Independence. People must remember these things. We went through hell not because the British were resisting it, but the enemy was from within Saint Lucia.

Q: **What were some of the difficulties encountered returning to office in 1982 after the leadership struggle and the eventual collapse of the SLP Government?**

A: It was a hell of a job to rebuild due in part to Hurricane Allen in 1980 which flattened the country, as well as reestablishing constitutional rule because of the interim government that had set the date for the general election and to begin an economic program for rebuilding Saint Lucia. The leadership struggle cost us 5 years. People don't realize just how much it took to rebuild Saint Lucia and to bring it back from how we found it with the economy in ruins, schools broken down, health centers in disarray, all the services-it took a long time!

Q: **Sir John, your critics and even some of your supporters claim that you have a somewhat aloof demeanour and some argue that you are an extremely stubborn individual. Would that be an accurate characterization?**

A: Well, different people see different things in me. I was called a communist, I was called all types of things in my political career. I greet everybody. I walk the streets in Saint Lucia without a bodyguard. Probably I do not like this flattering of crowds, but that's me. Talking about stubbornness, I listen. If I have something to do I would knock it around with my friends, my close associates and after I have listened to them, I make up my mind. Look! Everything I've done, I've met obstruction: some from the SLP, some from outside, Rodney Bay development. Do you remember when we were doing the dredging for the connection to Pigeon Island, all the obstruction? Even the road connecting Castries to Gros Islet, but my goal was to serve and to bring about positive change. The things that I've done are referred to as social engineering-to put shoes on people's feet, to put a proper roof over their heads, to bring electricity to their homes, to place their children in schools, and to bring them clean water. This was my objective in life.

Q: So decisions you have made, would you say they have been consensus decisions?

A: No! I can't say so. That would not be true. It's after I have knocked it around, listened to what others are saying, then I make up my mind. Now my one regret in politics, in government, is that I didn't listen to myself more, because now I know that the objectors had their own agenda to impede me from doing things. Some of them were in the senior branches of the government and are still there raking in the plums. There are a number of things I would have done. I look at the Castries harbour development and I see a number of things I should have done which have not been done and I don't know if they will ever be done, and I remember the obstruction. When I remember the government buildings in the Conway when my character was put into issue by people, in that case I did not back down. In the harbour development, I said to hell with them.

Q: As you go around the island you see the John Compton H/way, The Government Buildings on the waterfront, Pointe Seraphine, The Rodney Bay Marina and the Causeway. There must be a great sense of accomplishment not withstanding all the obstacles and criticisms that came your way?

A: Oh yes, these were the physical things. The things I am most proud of are the number of people who are now professionals, that I gave an opportunity to go to school. In every part of this country you see the uniform of a secondary school. When I came in, there were two secondary schools. Then after that I built the third (Vieux Fort Secondary School) when I was in the Labour government because I got the money from the American bases. I negotiated it to build that school and then the long gap and later 16, 18, probably 20secondary schools.

Q: **Walk us through what must have been a deeply emotional moment for you on the night of Independence in the company of British royalty and other heads of state.**

A: It would have been emotional yes! I was proud because it was one of my achievements. I was happy because of course you are free, I was sad because it was not the flag of the Caribbean countries that was being hoisted, not the West Indies flag.

Q: **And that had been priority for you?**

A: Yes! That was my priority, because I know looking down the road of history in 25 years from now, it would not be the same. I do not know that we can survive as a country with what is happening. We should have had the West Indies defenses around us to give us a response to what is happening in the world today. We are going to be overwhelmed. You have 5 million people, 15 prime ministers....five million people is a small city in England. I was sad that my goal was not accomplished to be part of a West Indian nation. So this was my emotion at the time, proud, happy, yet sad, mixed emotions.

Q: **Up to that time what could you say were the main achievements of the John Compton administration?**

A: I don't know what were the main ones because you have various aspects of the economy and one could not go without the other. The whole thing was a series of building blocks to create the nation. The nation was not born on February 22. The building of the nation probably started before you were born. Everybody, every generation must put a block. It started off in the 1930s when you had the Cooperative Bank and various associations in which, at last, the small black middle class started to emerge and the organization of our society of the rich man in the castle and the poor man at the gate, with nobody in the middle, that started to crumble. Then in the forties things started to change when people started having their own associations. We had the Agriculturists Association, the Coconut Growers Association, and the black middle class started emerging to challenge the supremacy of the existing order. Then came adult suffrage, the emergence of the trade unions.All of these are building blocks of independence. Then we had the 1957 sugar strike which broke the back of the existing order.

Q: And you were one of the stalwarts of that development?

A: Yes! I was one of the stalwarts, I was the catalyst. That is what broke the back of the existing order and caused the change to the banana industry which is now being destroyed. Then you had tourism, the schools and light manufacturing, all of these are part....for example people speak about tourism and I want them to understand. Here you have most of your tourists in the north of the island but your international airport for geographical and historical reasons is in the south. You have to connect the two points, so we had to build the east coast road, all of these are the small building blocks. When you think of housing, the ajoupa, the thatched roof mud hut had to go. The Urban Development Corporation was created for that purpose. It built Sans Soucis. All this was part of a progressive change that was being accomplished at that time. Look at water and how many children per thousand were dying because of water borne disease - dysentery, typhoid. One of my best friends, Maurice Mason, died from typhoid fever. He was representing Dennery at the time where there were high incidents of typhoid, but look at the changes now - water in every part of the community. The infant mortality rate here is on par with the United States because we brought water to the communities. So we cannot say it was this or that. It was a package of social change.

Q: Sir John, you led Saint Lucia through two spells for a total of 30 years. What would you say was the secret of your longevity?

A: In spite of all they say about my aloofness as you asked me just now and my arrogance, still people vote for you because they love you, because I have public support. I have left active politics now for nearly eight years and even now I am the subject of the commentators. Even now they try to tarnish me, they try to airbrush me out of history.

Q: How do you feel about that, they trying to airbrush you out of history?

A: They are like little boys throwing stones at the moon; you can never catch it.

Q: By the way, what is the real story about your relationship with Odlum and the country's big surprise that you would send him, your arch enemy to the UN?

A: It was embracing. My relationship with George goes back from childhood. We lived as neighbors and I was one of those responsible for getting him back home, then into a job at the WISA Secretariat, but he became involved with the forum and began attacking the very Prime Ministers that he was accountable to. He didn't contest the elections of 1992, so I said, perhaps George has mellowed. An opportunity came for me to appoint an Ambassador to the United Nations and I thought that he would have been an excellent choice, so I consulted with my colleagues. I couldn't say that I got unanimous support. I couldn't say that they embraced him, but they accepted my advice and he went to the UN and while there he served well. You see, Dave, there are some in my party, supporters even, who would say why this or that person, all of which creates a lot of unnecessary division. We're too much of a small country for that. I'm not choosing you because of the color of your shirt, but rather, the content of your character and your ability to do the work.

Q: Political pundits have been mystified by the fact that you never identified a successor from within your own party, so it came as a surprise when you handpicked Dr. Vaughan Lewis, an outsider, to succeed you as Prime Minister.

A: You are right. I asked him to come in to be Prime Minister. I never expected the UWP to lose the 1997 elections.

DS: **Ah! but some people have said that you knew you were going to lose. Hence the reason why you retired and threw him literally to the wolves so to speak.**

A: No! No! No! I have never lost and I would not have lost. I didn't invite him to serve in opposition. I looked down the road to see what kind of Prime Minister we would need in the era of the World Trade Organization, Globalization and Emerging Economics, to interface with the leaders of the world who were versed in these areas, to stand up for Saint Lucia in this sort of environment. I expected him as Prime Minister to bring all his knowledge and experience to bear in these sorts of negotiations. I didn't invite him in to keep meetings in Des Barras and shout out in Oleon. That was not the role I saw for him. Special times need special types of people. The times I had foreseen needed a person like him. If I was looking for someone to do street fighting, I might have had second thoughts, but I never expected us to lose in 1997. I thought here was a person with the experience, knowledge and contacts to bring to the table.

Q: **There is a feeling that Dr. Lewis should have called a snap election after he won the by-election in Central Castries, because the Labour Party was in disarray at that point. What kind of political pressure would you have brought to bear on him by virtue of the fact that you were the former leader?**

A: No! No! it was his prerogative. He was the one to choose the date.

Q: **If you had the opportunity to lead Saint Lucia again, is there anything you would do differently?**

A: I told you, I would listen more to myself. I don't know what I would have done differently. There are some things I would have liked to have done. I do not have the opportunity so I am not going to cry over it. You know, people like to tar you with a brush and whatever you do, some of the paint remains, like me being stubborn and arrogant and all of this. The fact is I don't like people trying to interfere with my character because I think that's the only thing my parents gave me besides my education.

Q: Any rancour?

A: No! I have no rancour, no regrets. I have done my bit, I have served my time. I look back and I have a certain measure of satisfaction with what I have done. My only regret is to see that a number of things that I have done now being undone, My regret is to see that a lot of people who followed me from the time I started, now being kicked around and being victimized and I cannot do anything to defend them. My regret is to see when I drive on the roads on an afternoon, going to the country in my little pick-up truck, to see the hundreds of children walking, when part of the social engineering we tried to perform was to take them from their homes to the schools and back to their homes. These are regrets.

Q: Any final thoughts?

A: I've said all I've got to say. I've opened my heart to all, but I just want to thank the people of Saint Lucia for allowing me to serve. That's been my greatest satisfaction of having served and hopefully served well.

The following story on Sir John, was related by former cabinet minister in his administration (1982-1996) Mr. Louis George, who was interviewed by David Samuels on the Program "The Agenda" on RSL 97, just a few days before the state funeral of the former Prime minister.

Some overseas visitors came to the PM's office insisting that it was imperative they saw him, as they were just in for the day. Mr. George informed them that the PM was in his constituency all day and to take them there would necessitate an hour's drive. They said that they didn't mind the trip as it was important.

Says Louis "As soon as I drove up the hill towards the estate house, I noticed Sir John climbing an avocado tree, and with a stick in his hand was trying to pick some avocados and at the sound of the car he turned and acknowledged me, Louis! He exclaimed, I said "Yes Sir! I brought you some people who would like to see you", He said "OK! Take them inside". The people in the car queried, "Who is that man?" I responded, "This is the man that you've come to see", and the visitors could not contain their surprise, if not disbelief. They said "You're not serious?" And I said "Yes! This is the Prime Minister of Saint Lucia!"

Continued Louis "I took them to the house and the PM came through a back door moments later; rubber boots on, an old torn shirt with his tummy out, an old cap on his head and he sat down and said "Hello! What can I do for you?" and while engaging the still shocked visitors in a discussion, ate a piece of cooked breadfruit and copra from a plate on the table in the room".

I looked at him, laughed and thought. "Boy! This is the man for you!" He had no inhibitions about being on the estate and caring about what people thought.

Another time, says Louis, I wanted to see him urgently and after a brief search, found him in a pig pen with a broken shovel that could not have done the job effectively. PM used his hands to clean the pigs mess. That was the man Saint Lucians came to know and love.

The preceding comments on Sir John were made by former Cabinet Minister in his administration (1982-1996). Mr. Louis George, was interviewed by David Samuels on the Program "The Agenda" on RSL 97, just a few days before the state funeral of the former Prime minister. Mr. George passed away on 2nd of January, 2014, due to diabetic complications.

Sir John retired from politics in 1996, but returned to the fray in 2005, to lead his United Workers Party back into the seat of power in the 2006 elections and became Prime Minister again for the last time. He died on 7th September, 2007, at the age of 82 years.

The following note is from Lady Compton to the writer:

When we lost John, there were so many memorials to attend, so many letters to write and so many depressing things to attend to. I found myself leading to a place that I could not afford to go to, and so for my own sanity, I had to step back for a while.

So it's all the wonderful gestures of friendship, caring and concern that helped us through one of the most dreadful times of our lives. You went to such lengths and your beautiful letter will always be treasured. Bless you for the part you played, we shall always remember your caring.

With the passing years, there has been much time for reflection, much time to observe others and more and more I realize what an exceptional human being my husband was. His simplicity, his humility, his attitude-never believing he was perfect, but, here I am, take me as I am, without the need for trimmings and trappings-for whom material things meant nothing unless they were essential, a man without an ounce of vindictiveness. A man whose almost childlike joy was in seeing something he thought was for the benefit of Saint Lucia come to fruition and all this, despite the many years of abuse and criticism. John Compton was truly rare and I was so privileged to have walked by his side for forty years and be a witness to all that he was and all that he achieved for Saint Lucia and for Saint Lucians.

Sir John Monument:

A 9' Bronze Freedom Image in honor of Sir John was installed by the Saint Lucia Government on February 21st, 2014, as part of Saint Lucia's 35th anniversary of Independence.

The Monument is appropriately displayed in the Constitution Park, and depicts Sir John, his right hand raised holding the new constitution of the country on its attainment of Independence; the Parliament building is to the right, while the halls of Justice are to the left. The Life-like depiction faces the William Peter Boulevard, which is home to Sir John's UWP, (since its inception in 1964) and which also houses the John Compton office building. The Castries Constituency Council Building on Peynier Street serves as a backdrop to the monument.

There still continues to be debate among political pundits and observers, as to why the Stephenson King-UWP led administration would have allowed its term to elapse without the launching of the monument. Writes Earl Bousquet "That honor was being paid to Sir John by an SLP administration, after his own party in office, failed to raise and erect it from its long slumber." The KDA Administration needs to be commended for this bold and welcome initiative.

At that official installation ceremony were Governor General Dame Pearlette Louisy, Prime Minister Dr. Kenny D. Anthony and his wife, Rosemary Belle Antoine, Sir John's family including Lady Janice Compton and their children and grandchildren, Parliamentarians on both sides of the isle, old party faithfuls like Ira D'auvergne, Cyril Landers, Ferdinand Henry, Hollis Bristol among others and for many years the party's secretary Mrs. Gertrude George. Also in attendance was Dr. Keith Mitchell- Prime Minister of Grenada, dignitaries from the region and members of the general public. It was undoubtedly the highlight of Independence activities for that year. The monument is the work of sculptor Ricky George.

CHAPTER 13

A CONVERSATION WITH DR. KENNY D. ANTHONY

"Optimist"

I hold very dearly the interviews I've conducted throughout my career with Prime Ministers of Saint Lucia. I interviewed Kenny Anthony three times as Prime Minister. The first was in 2004 on the occasion of Saint Lucia's 25th anniversary of Independence, along with other former Prime Ministers: Sir John Compton, Mikey Pilgrim, Allan Louisy, Winston Cenac and Dr. Vaughan Lewis. The second time was a year later on "Coffee Break at Sandals La Toc", and the last at the Sandals Halcyon, just one week before the December 11, 2006 general election.

I've always found Dr. Anthony a somewhat challenging interviewee because he always seemed to exude an aura of superiority as though wanting to dictate or control how the discussion should flow. He would persistently test you and if you were not alert, he could easily throw you off your comfort zone. He would usually butt in and interject before you could complete your questions, challenging you as to their veracity and when attempting to respond, he would speak all over you in what appeared to be a form of intimidation to overwhelm the interviewer. Seldom have I encountered such a challenge in my broadcasting career.

I don't know if it was because some party members had fixed a political label to me for all sorts of dubious reasons. The most ridiculous of all was the claim that I had secured a bank loan for my business, then used it for the election campaign of the United Workers Party. The truth is that, during the Castries Bye Election campaign of 1996 and the General Election campaign of the following year, the UWP had brought in their consultants from Barbados and Trinidad to assist in running their campaigns and DSP video facilities was only commissioned to produce material for the campaigns. As the saying goes "I was just ketching a work!" I suffered much, as tens of thousands of dollars owing to me were never paid, coupled with the ostracization from the other side. Those were extremely painful, unforgettable and learning experiences.

So my December 6, 2006 interview with KDA was eagerly anticipated and broadcast live on Radio Saint Lucia just five days before the general election. Earlier that week Roger Joseph, the General Manager at Radio Saint Lucia had insisted that I submit a list of questions for the Prime Minister for his consideration. That morning I welcomed the PM at the hotel entrance and we strolled together up the stairs to the makeshift broadcast area just to the right of the swimming pool. As we approached the sitting area, Dr. Anthony suddenly blurted out loudly: "Oh Boy! That's a flambeau place!" You can well imagine my shock and discomfort, completely thrown off for a few moments. You see, the table which was laden with the usual treats for our invited guests: tea, coffee, juices, water, croissants, bread, cakes and a variety of delicacies, was laced and covered with a yellow table cloth and though I had been there for a while before the PM's arrival, I had not even recognized this, nor had my technical operator, Georgie. I just responded "PM! I have absolutely nothing to do with what color tablecloth the hotel chooses to use during the weekly programs" I could not believe that the PM would have reacted to the color yellow on such an innocuous item as a tablecloth. I was dumbfounded and embarrassed at how visibly upset and red in the face our PM had become. Maybe, I thought, it had more to do with the tremendous pressure he must have been under, trying to seek a third consecutive term, but undoubtedly the most serious and contentious battle since coming into office in 1997, being challenged by the 81 year old Sir John, back from retirement and he

KDA being 25 years his junior. Thus it was against this backdrop that the interview was conducted.

As to the actual interview, we covered a range of topics like the Rochamel Affair, Saint Lucia Media, Universal Health Care, Universal Secondary Education, The future of Catholic assisted schools, Tourism and Agricultural Development, Crime, Urban Development among other things. Some of the highlights follow:

DS: I would like to begin with some banter. Let's listen to the following calypso musical clip.

When talking 'bout country
St. Lucia is best
When talking 'bout country
We different from the rest
While most other countries
Have just one leader
We have two leaders in Saint Lucia

Kenny made one step forward with employment
Tony made two steps backward, six months back on the pavement
Kenny remove the license fee to drive on the road
Tony raise the price of gas which is a heavier load
Kenny give mini buses special concession
Tony raise up the cost of their operation

We have two people running this country just you wait and see
We have two people running this country I hope you can agree
We have two people running this country just look carefully
We have two people running the country Kenny and Tony...

DS: There's a strong body of opinion out there that you seem to display somewhat of a dual personality and the calypso enforces that notion.

A: It's an absurdity but a clever calypso! You have to take calypso for what it is and give the calypsonian credit for it. This is a Red Plastic Bag composition that found its way to Saint Lucia and to Bingo. The suggestion that you're dealing with is absurd really and of course, provided good fodder to my opponents. I think that there are things you take in stride and like I said, it's not an original but nonetheless, a cleverly written calypso. Yes! and I know that you love that song!

DS: Yes! Played it a few times...

There has been this pervasive atmosphere within the country that the SLP is paramount to the party - a sense that party is more important than Government, even country and we heard something like that from your Chairman, Tom Walcott in 2004.

A: I really don't know why you would want to resurrect that point but let me say this: The constitution of Saint Lucia is the supreme law of the land. No party can be above that and a government takes its cue from the constitution of the country. A party cannot disobey the constitution of the country. In my view, Tom Walcott was trying to make a very simple point: a government has to be elected and there will always be an umbilical relationship between government and party and he was issuing a warning that if you try to remove yourself from the policy as articulated by the party, when it comes to renewing your mandate, you will find yourself so alienated from your supporters and the voters that there is the possibility that they may disown you in a general election.

DS: Can't help but observe that you take my comments and questions sort of personally, as though you resent being asked them. I'm putting them to you because its being debated in public and I would hope that I am a voice, if not one of the voices, attempting to share some of their perspectives with you, Sir.

A: I don't agree with that! I think you are your own voice and I imagine that you are saying...

DS: **(Cuts In) I'm not! I'm not! I'm not imagining anything. I'm simply asking you some questions and you are being very testy with me this morning.**

A: Not at all! Not at all! I'm very interested in your interview and I'm not here to quarrel with you Dave...and I'm giving you the freedom to ask any question that you'd like to ask Dave, very late like I've said, but I'm happy to be here (laughs). In fact I'm quite generous with you this morning.

Q: You are being generous?

A: Its been a long time since you've had me on your show and I've never understood why I've not received more invitations. Of all the radio stations, I get the fewest invitations from state owned RSL.

DS: Well um um...I'm very sorry to hear that!

A: Its just a bit odd!

DS: We recognize that you're a very busy man and...

A: (Cuts in again) Well I've never been too busy to do interviews (laughs) so I don't know how solid an excuse that is, but never mind, I'm here now so lets proceed.

Q: Thanks! What has your relationship with the media been of late. There's been a feeling that you've had this almost rapturous love affair with the media, but not so of late. It seems to have soured... What has gone wrong Sir?

A: My Government has been exceedingly open with the media. Lets look at the facts. We've not closed down radio stations and have in fact increased the number of licenses, whether its radio or TV, but even more than this, no media manager, no commentator could say that this PM or a minister in his Government called them, begged for mercy and said don't do this or don't do that. We've allowed all and sundry to say what they want about the Government. Obviously, some of us reserve the right to sue people who engage in defamatory statements and that will always be the case. I myself have made it very clear that you can say what you want about me, but do not seek to damage my reputation, integrity or my character. I think its more important to understand what my underlying philosophy is about this matter. Basically, I believe the press and the Government should never lie on the same bed. They share different purposes in a democracy. The press have a right to search, to question, criticize. They live and work in a democracy and they have a right to express their views, but the Government in turn needs to clearly articulate public policy and it's bound to produce collision from time to time, and we exist to protect the expression of those views.

Q: It does not sound as though you're all that happy?

A: I would wish that more persons would be fair and more balanced and be concerned with veracity about things they say, but in the final analysis they have to be judged by what they say and do. There are persons in the press that I have great admiration for and, as normal, there are some who do a great job but there are others who cause disappointment from time to time. My only concern is that sometimes I find elements in the press who are exceedingly arrogant: they do not want to hear another point of view and they do not accept that politicians have a right to defend themselves. I don't think that's right. In as much as we allow such freedoms to exist, I think that when the press commits errors and exercises wrong judgment, they just do not want to be corrected. I find it is in the nature of the press to be like that.

Q: There's been a lot of debate about Universal Health Care (UHC) and Universal Secondary Education, (USE) I know that they are both challenging in implementation and financing. At what point are you, in their development and subsequent launch?

A: They are triumphant initiatives. We have reached out and attempted to modernize Saint Lucia with both of these initiatives. I'm exceedingly excited about USE because it means that every child in this country is guaranteed a place in a secondary school, but more than that, it would immediately increase the number of eligible persons for further education, particularly University education. I think that is key. I'm looking forward to the day when Common Entrance Examinations will be completely reformed. I also think that it will lay the basis to sort out the serious issue of the transportation of students away from their communities, and that is a huge burden for parents to bear. With UHC we've made some strides. Its been one of those burning and unfortunate issues. It is not right to deny people access to health care simply because they can't afford it. We have this horrible situation where we have to meet some of the costs of people who have to go overseas to receive medical attention. I particularly feel embarrassed at the numbers we have to send to Martinique, but nevertheless, grateful for that. I thank the French authorities, but at the same time, it must be a source of great embarrassment to us. We have taken a tentative step to UHC. There is still a long way to go because we have to set up the supporting infrastructure and we also have to resolve the issue of financing the initiative, but I believe that both of them, in the long term, will really benefit Saint Lucia as we have to modernize both our Education and Health services. I'm really very pleased by this and I'm glad that my Government was able to initiate those activities which will make a vital difference in the future of this country.

Q: **Your Government has been accused of being soft on crime. Is that a fair assessment?**

A: There can be no doubt that every Saint Lucian has a right to be concerned about crime, which is the number one agenda in every country in the Caribbean. It's a monumental task. I feel however that we should work hard to avoid politicizing crime. Crime is not an issue to be politicized. I feel strongly that both political parties need to work at it, to provide some sort of comfort levels to the society at large towards the issue, but the notion that my Government is soft on crime. What! You're going to judge a Government over hanging? That can't be the issue because the Government has to obey the law. The Government just can't go and hang anybody. It is the Courts that must clear the process by which hanging is to be carried out. A Government relies on a Police Force to implement the fight against crime. I know sometimes the police force lets us down but I also know that there are police officers who have worked extremely hard and are trying to stem the tide of crime. They are passionate and committed to it, and we cannot pretend that it is a recent thing. It has been in the making for years and now we have to confront the full reality and I believe that all citizens will really have to make the fighting of crime a national issue.

Q: Could you share some thoughts about the Tourism and Investment climate?

A: If we have to deal with our unemployment problem, we have to bring investment into the country as much as possible. To ask an investor to come and build in this country and spend US$200M - US$300M and tell them that all we can offer you is a lease on the property for 30/40 years? You're not going to get any investor putting up that kind of money on property, so we have to be realistic. You either want the investor or you don't. Thus the Alien Landholders Licenses for would-be investors is important and we have the power to grant those licenses. We have to continue to push tourism in the short term because there is room for growth, there is room for development and we have a number of investments on the way that will increase substantially the room capacity to which you referred. The policy is to continue the investment thrust in new hotels, while jealously guarding the patrimony of the people of Saint Lucia. We need to strengthen the linkages between tourism and agriculture, as we are still utilizing too little of what we produce for the hotels. We have to correct that.

Q: The Catholic Church today is in a struggle to remain an influential partner in education. We have managers who are generally figureheads as the decisions are being made by the Ministry of Education. In 1996 there were 57 schools managed by the C.E.B.M (Catholic Education Board Of Management). Today, there are 33. In recent times government has accelerated the pace to reclaim assisted schools. This policy is based on the ownership of schools and not...

A: (Cuts in) Can you give me evidence of what you are talking about because I'm a little lost? You say that the government has accelerated a policy to reclaim assisted schools? I need help on that matter...

DS: It's a Catholic document that I refer to...

A: (Cuts in) Can you give me an idea where this document came from and who is its author? just for the purpose of factual accuracy...

DS: It's Catholic information and directly from the...

A: (Cuts in) If you refer to the document and its author, then it will be analysed carefully.

DS: I have the document here (shuffling through papers) and its from the church – CEBM (the Catholic Education Board of Management)

A: Oh! that's helpful, ok!

Q: ...as I was saying, that policy is based on the ownership of schools and ignores the historical contribution of the Catholic Church, which has made a significant contribution to the development of schools since 1859.The decision to redesignate schools as government or Catholic assisted schools, has created a feeling that your administration's policy ignores the rights of parents to send their children to a school of their choice and it violates the principle that parents are the primary educators of their children.

There's concern too, that the Catholic character at some schools is disappearing and overall, Catholicism is being neutralized by your administration. Can you comment?

A: Totally unfounded! The majority of persons in my cabinet are Catholic, are strong believers in their faith and they, like everybody else, jealously protect their rights to religious freedom. Now I have to acknowledge the extraordinary contribution that the church has made towards education in much the same way that I acknowledge the extraordinary contribution by the Anglican Church in its early life made to education. You may have heard of the "Lady Mico schools" that were established by that church, initially to provide education to the emancipated slaves in the early years? The Riviere Doree Anglican School, was one of the first schools built from funds secured from the Lady Mico Charity after emancipation in 1834. There can be no doubt that the landscape has changed. There was a time when the Church could build schools relatively cheaply, find money, raise money, but that is no longer the case. The Church itself is under immense pressure to maintain existing plants. It's simply a reflection of the changing times and the changing circumstances, so that inevitably the burden of establishing new plants has fallen very squarely on the government of Saint Lucia, on the public purse. Even the church itself has had to turn to the government to provide financing to maintain existing plants. A case in point is St Mary's College, owned by the church, but it is the government that has financed the major expansions at the school. True, it raised some funds but it was the government that stepped in. For my part, I think it is right to have a diversified system of education. I believe it's important for parents to continue to have choices, but I also recognize that this has to be done in an ordered way and ordered fashion. We have to accept too that our society has changed substantially and a Government has a duty to be fair to all citizens.

Let's face it! At one time Saint Lucia was 80-90 percent Catholic, but this is no longer the case. We now have what can best be described as a very pluralistic society. Yes! Catholics are in the majority but you have Anglican, Seventh Day Adventists, Methodist, Pentecostal, etc. and a Government has to be fair to all and sundry. There's also the situation where the government has rebuilt some schools on church lands, so the church has raised the issue, "that because it's built on our lands, then it's our schools. On the other hand you have a situation where the Government built new schools on property owned by it and paid for the buildings and the Church says it is a replacement for a Catholic School, and therefore it should continue to be managed by the Church. Added to that you hear Church officials say that the former Government promised them this or promised them that or told them this or that, so there are all those issues and what the education act has done is to provide a mechanism to iron out those issues so that the state knows exactly what schools are within its domain, likewise the Catholic Church, SDA, Anglican etc., so that there is no dispute, but inevitably those things take time and I know there have been discussions about all of that, but I'm certain that it will all be worked out in due course, for I know that discussions have been ongoing for some time now."

DS: Sarah Flood-Beaubrun is still standing by her story that you disallowed prayers in cabinet.

A: Utter rubbish! Let me make my point very clear.

Q: So was she lying?

A: Yes! Yes! Yes! There are individuals of different religious persuasions in this country. I'm not a Catholic, I'm Anglican but I've admired the Catholic Church greatly. I've said so repeatedly. But I believe that the government has a right to protect the religious persuasion of its people. No one has a right to force their religious beliefs on other persons. It is wrong!

Q: And you think that she's done that?

A: I believe that individuals have a right to come to conclusions about their faith. There has never been a tradition of saying prayers in cabinet....

So ends the 2006 Coffee Break session, but I thought it would be appropriate to include his responses to questions on Saint Lucia's Independence which was recorded in 2004, as part of a series of programs with the Prime Ministers of Saint Lucia.

Q: During Independence celebrations every year, there's a certain degree of apathy in some quarters, rather than the unity that's generally associated with such an important national milestone. What have you done or are doing to unify the nation?

A: We are very hard on ourselves, so much so we do not see the real progress that we've made, the things we have achieved. All we do is to identify the weaknesses, the ills. Of late I have seen a far greater togetherness among the people than has been seen in the past. The UWP's have demonstrated a sense of ownership about independence because they attained it, that it doesn't belong to the labour party, because the SLP opposed it, although my government has been very different where that is concerned. We must really get both parties to work on similar issues of public interest, issues that dominate, that are larger than the political parties, but critically and crucially in our culture, that is to say in what we read, in what we write, in our music, in our churches. In our social institutions we have to preach unity more often. I think it is vital that our people understand that there can be political differences. Some of us can have another point of view but you respect that point of view. You respect that individual and you do not necessarily have to display any anger about it. It is part of the process of maturity and one of the things we have to concede to the political process, is its incremental maturity. I believe that we are moving in that direction, but what we need to do is to expedite it.

Q: And finally, some thoughts about nationhood and what you would like to see?

A: Independence belongs to all of us. It belongs to the country. It is the greatest gift that a country could possibly have had, but I would also say that we all need to recognize everybody's contribution and role towards its attainment. We have a habit of ignoring those who have contributed. The fact of the matter is that you could not have moved into independence in 1979 without decolonisation and the person who was responsible for commencing that process was George Charles. He's been completely forgotten. It's almost a case of historical amnesia, that our generation has been taught to forget what transpired between 1951 and 1961, and the immense amelioration that took place during that period so that was what PM Compton at the time inherited, were changes already ushered in by a then labour party administration which had become moribund because of internecine warfare among other reasons. I would want to say that there is a proper appreciation of the role of all parties, all individuals to that process....

Some Personal Reflections

I knew KDA as a teenager coming around the CDC area in the 60's at the apartment of "Miss Fannybell" and "Clinton Octave" at Block W Apt. 10. During that period he lived on the top floor of the Wallace Sanchez Building on the corner that is now the Vendors Arcade on Jeremie Street. As youngsters Clinton, Larry Daniel, a few others and I visited him regularly and patronized the shop operated by Sanchez on the ground floor. A few years later, as a teacher, KDA moved to the corner of High and Chisel Streets, which the Zayad Building now occupies. I lost contact with him for many years but was always happy to hear news about him from Clinton and Kate whenever I dined with them in New York throughout the eighties and early nineties. It was during one of those trips that I learnt that he was the Godfather of one of their children.

KDA has to be recognized for his academic and professional achievements and on holding the position of Prime Minister for nearly 15 years. He seemed to not only tolerate, but may have been influenced by some of the "advisors" around him, who fed him whatever he wanted to hear because their very survival depended on him remaining as Prime Minister. They had views on everything and on everyone, as overnight, they had become armchair experts and Kenny seemed to have bought into it. It played out as the classic "Emperor's New Clothes" Syndrome.

CHAPTER 14

A CONVERSATION WITH ALLEN M. CHASTANET

"PRAGMATIST"
Prime Minister of Saint Lucia (from June 2016)

On 6th June, 2016, Allen Michael Chastanet became the eighth person to occupy the position of Prime Minister of Saint Lucia since the island attained its Independence in 1979. Widely known in the tourism sector, he is the son of prominent businessman Michael Chastanet. Before becoming Prime Minister, the younger Chastanet had served as Minister of Tourism and Civil Aviation in Sir John Compton's cabinet and upon his passing, also served in the Stephenson King administration.

Mr. Chastanet owns a hotel and has interests in a tourism pleasure cruise operation, an obvious indication as to his strong belief and support for the industry.

Allen Chastanet's ascendency to the leadership of Saint Lucia was not an easy one beginning in his own UWP where he fought off three challenges in as many years while the party was in opposition, but he won overwhelmingly on all occasions. When this was over, he had to face a barrage of criticism from the then ruling Saint Lucia Labour Party which seemed to question everything about him even his intellect and suitability to lead the country on a range of spurious grounds including his race. The interview with Prime Minister Chastanet took place a few days after the 38th Anniversary of Saint Lucia's Independence at the Prime Minister's Office and another, shortly before Christmas, 2017.

Q: Let's go back a few years to 2006. How did you react when you received a call from Sir John inviting you to become a Cabinet Minister in his Government?

A: He said he'd like to make me Tourism Minister. Would I be willing to come on board. My family members supported the decision for me to go into politics. I still think we've not done enough to get people to appreciate how tourism works and the importance of marketing. I still hear people saying that when we spend money on marketing, that's money that could be used for the hospitals, education or building roads etc. Tourism is what's generating the income for Saint Lucia so it's tourism that is paying for those things. I think within the government, I have been able to show that tourism is a science and we can predict fairly accurately what our arrivals are likely to be based on: the amount of airline seats that we have; what is happening economically; how much money that we are spending, and doing so in a targeted way.

Q: Speak about your elevation to the leadership of the UWP after its defeat at the General Elections of 2011?

A: Leadership isn't something that you can aggressively pursue. It comes to you. It wasn't something that I presumed would ever happen. Clearly, after we lost the election and my unsuccessful bid to represent the Soufriere/Fond St. Jacques constituency, the position that I was interested in was the chairmanship of the party, which I thought would have given me the opportunity to remain in my business, yet still be involved in politics.

If you go back to 1997 when the party was decimated at the polls and again four and a half years later in 2001, it had to take the 81 year old Sir John return the UWP back into office. I got involved in that campaign somewhat late, sat in cabinet and had a front row seat so to speak to everything that was unveiled for the next five years. Sir John selected people who could win their seats. As I remember it, there wasn't that level of cohesion and agreement on the way forward but there was certainly consensus that Sir John should be the leader. When he died and with the emergence of King as political leader, it was very apparent that he had a huge task, principally because he wasn't elected by the populace but from within the party and maybe he felt compromised as a result of this and couldn't have taken a stronger stance against those people who had objections with moving in a new direction.

When we lost the 2011 General Election, I felt that the party needed to re engineer itself. Clearly, the electorate had demonstrated the loss of confidence in us, even though Labour narrowly won Babonneau and Gros Islet by two and seven votes respectively. So we commissioned a report which highlighted some of the weaknesses, in particular, that the UWP seemed to have difficulty in confronting the Frederick Visa issue head on and so, was there any justification in keeping him and if not, what would his future role be? Some people didn't accept that he was an impediment to the party's chances at the polls so that attempts at restructuring the party were being thwarted. However, some of us got together and decided that we needed to change the leadership or work towards forming a new party but time was against us and that seemed like a really huge challenge given the failure of third political parties in the past.

So a decision was made to challenge King as party leader. Several people were approached but they all turned down the offer and when asked if I would be interested, I agreed under two conditions.

1. That I would be guaranteed the support of at least eleven constituencies and 2. That if anyone wanted to change their support for me at anytime, they were quite free to do so but should first have a meeting advising me of this and I would leave. I didn't want to be ousted in an embarrassing and disrespectful manner.

After they accepted these conditions, we put together an effective group of people, a slate of executive members which became known as the A team and went around the country campaigning as a team. It was imperative that we showed supporters that we were cohesive and serious about the reorganization of the party. We won 13 of the 17 constituencies at the 2013 National Convention and shortly after we went on a retreat at which 90 people attended,(a cross section of supporters island wide) and created a 'mission values vision' and once that was accepted by all within the party, I was confident that we were ready for elections.

The essential thing was to take what Sir John had started, modernize it and move forward in the restructuring of the party with a strong focus on the constituency branches. There was an old saying at the time, that the "UWP was just an election machine that went to sleep soon after election". Well that's how it seemed to have been when Ghiraudy was the chairman. Clearly, that could no longer be the approach. We began organizing fund raisers which helped develop camaraderie between the branches and constituencies, as well as introduce policy guidelines and that was our mantra going into the next two party conventions, when I was challenged by Dr. Claudius Preville and Sarah Flood-Beaubrun in 2014 and 2015 respectively. Those conventions really helped solidify our base and confirmed in most people's minds that we were serious as a vehicle for change in the country.

Complementing this new thrust were the Gas Tax March, the Constituencies Expenditure Case pursued by the SLP Government and the Constituency Boundaries Issue in which we were taken to Court. Those were all very important issues and to the dismay of the Government, galvanized support for our party and a lot of people who had distanced themselves from us and the SLP, began feeling that we had become a serious force and started leaning towards us.

Even some hard core naysayers began coming around and so when King, Spider and others were firmly back on board, it was the People's

Parliament on the Wm Peter Boulevard that really reinforced in the minds of the electorate that the UWP was ready. It was that massive turnout on that evening that really set the stage for the election. Also, there was strong national resentment at the conduct of the former speaker and his manner at humiliating certain members of the opposition whom he would deliberately taunt and interrupt during their contributions in the House, so we set up the People's Parliament outside of the House and it worked. *(See parliamentary notes at the end of the chapter.)*

We took the Government to task on VAT, The Juffali and Impacs controversies, low police morale, the broken health sector and delayed promised opening of the two new hospitals, the reduction in subsidies, the rising unemployment especially among the youth, the decrease in tourist arrivals, the broken Court and Education systems, the negative growth rate and demoralizing mood in the country, the poor state of the roads and the unconscionable increase in vehicle license fees etc, some of which seemed to have impacted the most vulnerable in the society so that when we launched "5 to Stay Alive", and assured people that we had the capacity to turn around the economy and that we would be a Government of Compassion and Empathy, the cry became "Let's give Chastanet a chance!"

Q: **The Governing Labour Party's assault on the Chastanet family is well documented, which intensified after you became the UWP Political Leader. How were you able to cope? Your race and unsuitability for leadership were constantly the subject of derision on the lips of key SLP leaders and their surrogates.**

A: The assault on me as well as my father started before that. They took digs at me when I was Tourism minister and certainly when I ran in Soufriere. Interestingly, the last four to five nights before the 2011 General Election, the leadership of the SLP was anchored in Soufriere and the attacks were relentless. All kinds of allegations were made about my father's supermarket chain dominating the economy. When I took over the leadership, it became more vicious and outrageous in terms of what they were alleging. For me, when I see people getting that low into the gutter, it signifies a level of desperation and so I never felt the need to respond and I was certainly encouraged by the number of phone calls and by people whom I met, who themselves were incensed by what was being said on the SLP platform. I felt that in many ways they were feeding red meat to their base (pardon the pun) but the independent and swing voters were unimpressed and my UWP base was resolute in its support for me.

Q: You've not commented though on the race card, your economic background and of you not being too conversant in Kweyol, yet running in a partially rural kweyol speaking constituency?

A: My father always kept me very grounded and has always felt that one needs to earn his own way. He never gave me any special treatment. On his cargo ships I worked as a stevedore in the engine room and did everything needed that the other Saint Lucian workers had to do and that was how I was able to pay my way to university. When Dad became more financially and economically successful, it didn't change my lifestyle and of my being able to relate and communicate with the ordinary man in the street, the market vendors and the farmers and fishers in the rural communities, most of whom spoke in Kweyol. During my vacation, I played regular basketball with the guys in the gardens, as I'd rather be there than with the so called "jetset" in the north.

All the jobs I've had, as an economist working with Sir John, Ausbert D'auvergne and Sir Dwight, regional public and private sector administrators too, but probably the greatest education for me was at Air Jamaica with Butch Stewart and the PJ Patterson Jamaica Government at the time. People have always underestimated my ability to connect with others but that connection began a very long time ago, so politics has been an easy transition. Even when Kenny won the election of 1997 (16-1) I was tipped to become his Tourism Minister.

Q: **Really? This is the very first time that I've heard of this!**

A: Oh really? I've mentioned this before. I just felt that I could have done more for him and Saint Lucia in my regional position at the time. I remember being introduced to Philip J. Pierre and Kenny asking me to assist him in any way possible.

Q: **What has challenged you the most about being Prime Minister?**

A: The expectation that the PM can do everything, and even though that may be potentially true, I certainly don't operate that way. I think it is dangerous that any entity as large as Government depends solely on one person so we've worked very hard to make sure that we understand and always obtain that level of consensus in cabinet and that is even in meeting the expectations of people. For instance, The 5 to stay Alive-Those were the things we wanted to accomplish in the first 100 days and we were able for the most part to do that, but then we inherited a budget and I had two options: spend time to redo the budget but I felt that by the time we had done so, we would have already been in a new budget cycle so it was better to work with the existing budget and to start the reconstruction process. We're working extremely hard and I really want to thank the public servants and the technocrats in particular for the time that they're putting in. I know how difficult it is for some of them to understand what we are trying to do putting this fiscal budget together and to begin the process of a four year strategic plan for the country. We also inherited a situation where people's contracts went way past the period of the elections. I was severely hampered in that regard dealing with boards that were appointed by the former administration and to get those members acquainted with the new direction, getting them in line with our thinking.

Q: **Since assuming office has there been any matter of significance that you wish to elaborate on?**

A: Its very difficult for me to say and I'll tell you why. I expected resistance and so I'm not disappointed. Some of the people we met there were defiant and made life unnecessarily difficult but there were others who expressed a desire to work with us because they realized that they couldn't work with the old policies. The other disappointment is the leaks of information. In trying to embarrass the Government, some are in fact undermining the structure of Governance in the country, not the UWP, but the Government itself. The Civil Service is intended to be independent and autonomous. Its work is for "All the people" and so they should be impartial. Those levels of leaks create distrust which is unnecessary so I've done my best in not reacting to that.

Q: **Returning to tourism just a bit. Why is it that after some 50 years there has not been more acceptance? If anything, there continues to be lingering suspicions about the industry. Why is this so and what can you do to change the narrative?**

A: That problem isn't only here in Saint Lucia but is constantly being debated throughout the Caribbean. This is the most tourism dependent region in the world, yet you would have thought that there would be more expertise residing here given our dependence and how important tourism is. Yet there isn't, whether it's from banking, consulting or education. Can you name a top Caribbean Tourism University? The difficulty is that people have not understood the broad reaching effects of tourism because we have failed to take advantage of its many opportunities. We've grown to depend on the bigger hotels because it's more challenging for the smaller properties to prosper and governments too have failed to create the environment to give nationals and other people in the region the opportunities to succeed and that's why we want to change that with our Village Tourism concept.

We're creating a franchise so that anybody who wants to operate a Food Bed and Breakfast (FB&B) facility, a home stay program, a small Bed and Breakfast (B&B), Liquor store or Gift shop, will apply to become a member of Village Tourism and if you're lacking the requisite skills, we're going to give you recommendations for training. We're going to provide the accounting systems, the marketing platform, source the towels, soaps and other products for you so that there is a consistent standard. We're also going to acquaint you with the health standards required which will be continuously available and what all of this does is change the mindset of the banking institutions that have lost faith in those small businesses, so that they will be encouraged to provide loans because all of a sudden they're not dealing with just that person by themselves anymore but someone who is now part of a concept with a support mechanism. We are going to spend US$30-40M on the physical improvement of several fishing villages. We will begin with Gros Islet and Soufriere but the concept will include Anse La Raye, Canaries, Choiseul, Laborie, Dennery Village and Micoud North. We also want to enhance the Castries Market, in collaboration with the Castries Constituency Council, to ensure that the products being sold there are more in harmony with our Saint Lucianness. "Vendors are not artisans: they are marketeers". We will ensure that visitors to our shores, along with residents, will be able to go to a revamped new market and will be able to find a much wider range of products that will be attractive to them.

Q: Given all of that, do you think that the day will soon come when the general citizenry will see tourism as not just foreigners visiting our shores, but view the industry as providing services like any other business?

A: Well our people must be made to understand that it's the fastest growing industry in the world and has been the most resilient over any other industry. We need a critical mass. We need more hotel rooms if we are to continue to attract more airline seats and by extension more flights into the island which would help make us more competitive in the marketplace. We've got our work cut out for us in taking away the servitude connotation. Service is service whether you are a bank teller, receptionist, vendor or grocer. We have to always strive to deliver service professionally. Another thing! Its been said in some circles that the white managers exploit the country and its people. Now there may have been a few examples of that but look at the number of hotels and small properties that are Saint Lucian owned? 99% of the people working in the hotels and in the industry are Saint Lucians. I think that a lot of the negativity is politically motivated because Allen Chastanet is a former Tourism Minister and now the Prime Minister. That's what it's all about but I'm not working for me but for the people of Saint Lucia and the generation now and those in the future will eventually savor the fruits of our hard work. It's for us to create a brand in Saint Lucia that's world class and when you have a strong brand you become more resilient. If I'm a good marketeer, I would obviously have to appreciate the culture and patrimony of Saint Lucia. Otherwise what am I selling? A very strong brand... Saint Lucia. Let her inspire you!

Q: **You've travelled extensively over the last few months, moreso after the passage of Hurricanes Irma and Maria, in an effort to reverse any potential economic slowdown as a result of those hurricanes. How successful have you been?**

A: When we came in we were very clear that there were three major impediments to growth in Saint Lucia: Infrastructure; the Airport is too small; the Seaport's too small; in addition there are not enough roads; we're not producing enough water and there's insufficient distribution of that precious commodity; and the sewage system needs urgent attention. Then, we've come to the realization that our education system has failed us. People are not trained to occupy the jobs that are available.

The Public Service: We need to re- engineer the public service where there is generally a lack of accountability. Civil Servants have realized for very long that we're only temporary in our position as a minister or a government and that may change in five years and so accountability is lacking. We have to take some bold steps to find out how much it would cost us to deliver a public service to the people of this country that is second to none.

Debt: If you do not fix the debt problem and constrain your expenditure, as you're growing and if your debt is growing with you, then you are making the problem worse. If in fact there's a downturn in the economy and your debt is high, then that undermines your ability to be successful.

So how are we going to resolve all of this? We have a plan for the Infrastructure, the Educational System and the Public Service and finally a plan for managing the debt. Then we have to start considering, "How are we going to attain direct foreign investment to start generating growth? We're looking at the revision of trade agreements with Mexico, Canada and the US, solving the problems that have emerged with the corresponding banking and derisking, which would have meant that Saint Lucians would not have been able to use their credit cards when they traveled and tourists would not have been able to use theirs as well and so we've moved very quickly with the Governor of the Central Bank and had a lot of meetings with the private sector in the United States to avert what would have been catastrophic".

Q: **Against the backdrop of all of the challenges you've outlined, we in the Caribbean, especially some of the neighboring islands, felt the impact of hurricanes Irma and Maria. How were you able to deal with all of this and could you indicate whether this will hamper in any way your economic projections for the island?**

A: A crisis is a horrible thing to waste and I knew that we had to move quickly to take advantage of the Global News cycle and as Chairman, we were able to collate as the OECS and come up with a four point strategy for Climate change and resilience building and financing, which were also addressed by myself and other Prime Ministers at the United Nations General Assembly. A major issue was that the Organization for Economic Cooperation and Development (OECD) classified Small Island Developing States (SIDS) as middle and high income countries on just per capita GDP coordinates, which would have made it difficult for us to gain access to concessional funds. Some of those meetings took me to Mexico, Canada, Morocco, Taiwan and elsewhere gaining their support, as well as the UK Government and everybody else, including the World Bank, were responsive. Hence we took advantage of the momentum all the way to COP 23 in Fiji. I've said all this to indicate that, if you want to sustain the foreign direct investment that you're getting into, you have to show that you have the ability to protect those investments and that's what resilience building is all about.

Q: **So how does Saint Lucia's Citizen by Investment Program (CIP) factor into all of this?**

A: It certainly has the potential to create a new source of revenue streams. It's really free capital to fuel economic growth and we will utlize that money to drive investment and/or pay off debt to stabilize the economy. A main focus is on due diligence as there are similar programs in some islands of the Organization of Eastern Caribbean States, (OECS) but I believe that due diligence is what separates one country from another and the fact that we are the new kid on the block, has taught us a few things about the mistakes that others have made. We are having some discussions about the harmonization of all those CIP's and I suspect that it's a conversation that will continue to take place for a while until some consensus is arrived at by the regional leaders. (Information about Saint Lucia Citizen by Investment Program is available online for those persons who are interested).

Q: **Speak to the level of investment that you anticipate over the next couple of years through to the end of your first term in 2021?**

A: We have been very successful in attracting huge investments. We are putting plans together and are all set to execute. We will commence the construction of the new Hewanorra Airport Terminal which is at least 10-15 years overdue and will also see the strategic investment in a Cruise Ship Terminal in the south, along with the construction of the horse racing track facilities and hotel park by Desert Star Holdings

(DSH) Also, there are going to be several new hotel developments in the island but particularly in the south and we're very excited about all of that. On top of this, agricultural production is on the increase and we're looking at investing millions of dollars in new feeder roads so as to help the farmers increase production of bananas and other crops. There will also be a focus on agro processing and the realization of the Hotel Chocolate Factory (pronounced Cho-co-la) as well as the reactivation of the Copra Factory in Soufriere. There will be a huge shift in the future operations of the Marketing Board and the full implementation of OJO Labs using artificial intelligence in an emerging industry, providing full time employment for some five hundred young people. Then there's the newly established "Headquarters Act" with several corporate regional businesses already making Castries City their headquarters, which creates new demand for Managers, Secretaries, Administrators, Accountants, Lawyers, etc. and the opportunity for Saint Lucians to provide apartments, office spaces, restaurant and bar services to facilitate this new thrust, which all adds to creating a new level of confidence in the country. Included is a massive road rehabilitation exercise and advances in health care, sporting and cultural facilities. The unemployment statistics are already trending downward and with all of the anticipated economic activity, I am optimistic that for the first time in many years that figure will assume single digit status. That's really my hope.

Q: **What message do you have for Saint Lucians in the Diaspora: US, Canada, UK, BVI, USVI, St. Marteen, French Antilles etc, many of whom speak of being forgotten and not wooed sufficiently in playing a bigger role in the economic, educational, social and cultural development of their country?**

A: We're opening our first Diaspora office in Miami to serve Saint Lucians in the United States. That office will be manned by officials of the Tourism Authority, Invest Saint Lucia, Foreign Affairs, Cruise and Hospitality personnel from a labor perspective. We will appoint Honorary Consuls General in some major US cities whose mandate will be to attend important meetings but who will liaise with the

Diaspora office who will provide all of the administrative backup in Miami. In due course we hope to replicate that model to include Toronto, Canada, and then London, England. We wish to extend those services as well to Saint Lucians in the BVI, USVI and St. Marteen. Since the passage of Hurricanes Irma and Maria, we've come to the realization that we need to connect with them more than ever before.

Q: **Any thoughts about the observance and celebration of our Independence and what it should signify for Saint Lucians at home and abroad?**

A: It's an opportunity for us to reflect on the things that we have achieved. Lets celebrate the fact that regardless of our differences and some of the problems we have, we've still made a mark in the world. Lets celebrate patriotism, highlighting and showcasing the positives about our land and the talent and excellence of our people.

- ➤ Two Nobel Laureates
- ➤ The Pitons-World Heritage Site
- ➤ Other World Renowned Sites
- ➤ Picturesque Yachting Marinas
- ➤ World acknowledged Music festivals
- ➤ Best Honeymoon Destination
- ➤ World Class Investments
- ➤ The most hospitable people in the region

Some of our athletes competing against the best in the world and holding their own. Lets put our differences aside and celebrate what's great about Saint Lucia. Lets also give recognition to those who've gone before us and those who've retired, all making their contribution towards the prosperity of this land for generations now and future generations to enjoy.

In conclusion, here are some excerpts from a Television infomercial produced for Allen Chastanet in the General Election of 2011 when he ran as a candidate for the Soufriere/Fond St. Jacques Constituency. The comments are from his wife, Raquel, and his father, Michael.

Raquel Chastanet:

Allen as a husband is terrific. He's very supportive of me personally and professionally and an absolutely fantastic and devoted father. I hear him articulating his thoughts daily. "These are the things that I want for Saint Lucia!" It can be difficult to marry personal time with professional time and I'm sure that politicians' wives long before me have had to confront some of those issues. I've always been struck about how much Allen loves Saint Lucia and how much he wants to do to propel the country forward-as a Man, as a Father, as a Husband and as a Saint Lucian. I knew Allen long before there was Allen, the politician.

Michael Chastanet:

Allen from young was a very outgoing individual. From a young boy Allen feared nothing. He would jump in the sea, into the deep water totally fearless. Allen is a people's person. He loves to raise people from the ranks and help make something out of them. He's really attracted to people and his focus in life is to make people's lives better. I hope that he embraces discipline and he must not take anything for granted. He has to always dot the I's and cross the T's and remember always that elections are won on election day.

PARLIAMENTARY NOTES:

The proceedings of the House of Assembly have been entrusted to a speaker who, in keeping with the Westminster Parliamentary tradition, is expected to regulate the conduct of business in the house. In so doing, the Speaker is empowered by the Standing Orders of the House, and where these orders fall short in any matter, the Speaker is bound to resort to the Westminster practice for guidance.

The Standing Orders that guide the Saint Lucia House of Assembly were made under the Constitution of Saint Lucia and were approved by the House of Assembly on 14 May, 1979. They give the Speaker the full authority to preside over the proceedings of the House, provided that the Speaker conducts himself within the rules of order. What this means is that there is no need for a Speaker to be contentious when engaging a Member of the House, because the Speaker simply has to apply the rules and direct the member accordingly. This posture is what inspired a quip among Commonwealth Parliamentarians in the 1990's, that "Speakers don't speak-they simply direct!". As amusing as this quip may sound, it speaks to a popular position among Commonwealth House Speakers, that a Speaker never gets involved in debate on the floor. Even when a Speaker is elected from within the ranks of elected parliamentarians, all he or she has under certain circumstances, is a casting vote.

It was therefore surprising at the last sitting of the House of Assembly, just prior to the June 6, 2016 General Election, to witness Mr. Speaker taking on the role of a prosecutor, as he probed the intentions of the Member for Castries South- East. The important question here must be: was the member in breach of any of the rules? And if for argument's sake, he was, Mr. Speaker simply had to guide him along the right path.

That particular display by Mr. Speaker not only went contrary to Parliamentary practice, but it also exposed the over zealous nature of the Speaker. The fact that Mr. Speaker is a lawyer by profession does not give him the right to interrogate members. If a rule is broken, let him point to such a fact and direct the member concerned accordingly. The Speaker must always be made aware of the need to preserve the traditions and the conventions of our Parliament and to constantly reinforce these practices for the sake of future Parliamentarians.

HONOUR ROLL

For Saint Lucia's independence in 1979, Minvielle and Chastanet gave the island an unusual gift: a series of national arts awards to be presented annually to the best artistes in the literary, visual and performing arts. I was delighted when in the tenth year of the awards DSP's production of "Sweet Sounds of Saint Lucia, 'Rameau' Joseph Poleon and band", was cited for an M&C Fine Arts Award. It was a signal honour that again thrust DSP into the national limelight.

This was just one of the several awards DSP and myself picked up in the ensuing years. Our complete list of awards reads like this:

1989: Minister of Information and Broadcasting Award for "Creative Advertising".

1989: Prime Minister's 10th. Independence Anniversary Award for "Creative Promotions". (A jingle with video footage, promoting SLU at 10).

1989: M&C Fine Awards

1990: Saint Lucia Media Awards for "Most appealing TV commercial" "Aqua Action"

1990: Saint Lucia Media Awards for "Best TV documentary" (second prize)

1991: Saint Lucia Media Awards for "Best Human Interest TV feature"

1993: National Service & Hospitality Awards for "Best Tourism media – A 15 minute weekly TV Production broadcast on HTS" for "Tourism is our business"

1996-97: National Service & Hospitality Awards "Best Tourism Media Production" for "Saint Lucia in your pocket". (a pocket size tourism publication targeting all in the tourism industry was available free at all hotels, resorts, restaurants, bars, boutiques, shops and tourist hangouts.

The phenomenal moment came in 2017 when I was nominated for a national award in the Independence Anniversary Honours List. The Saint Lucia Medal of Merit (SLMM) was given to me for "long and meritorious service in the field of Broadcasting". The actual presentation was made by Governor General Dame Pearlette Louisy at Government House on Sunday 26th February, 2017. The citation for the award went like this:

Mr. David Cletus Sinus Samuels

(For meritorious service in the field of broadcasting)

Mr. David Samuels has the distinction perhaps of being the longest serving member of the broadcasting fraternity in Saint Lucia. In a career that spans some 45 years, he has contributed significantly to the raising of standards in the profession and in providing avenues for media practitioners to launch their own businesses.

Mr. Samuels began as a rookie announcer with the Windward Islands Broadcasting Service (WIBS) in 1968. With the clear, clean, distinctive voice and impeccable diction that was the hallmark of announcers of the day, he was an instant hit with radio audiences in Saint Lucia and the Windward Islands. He would later work with Radio Caribbean International and Radio Saint

Lucia. His radio programmes including "Halcyon Quarter", "Coffee Break with Sandals" and "The Agenda" were all hugely popular.

He founded Dave Samuels Productions (DSP), becoming the first Saint Lucian to run a full service public relations and production company. There were television productions like "Tourism is your business", print publications like "St Lucia in your pocket" and music productions, one of which, the Rameau Poleon album of authentic Saint Lucian music earned him an M&C Fine Arts Award in 1989.

Dave Samuels remains active in broadcasting, appearing currently on his TV talk show, "Mr. Chairman". For his long service in the field of broadcasting. Mr. David Samuels is awarded the Saint Lucia Medal of Merit (Silver).

ACTIVITY LOG

1967-Teacher at the R.C Boys Primary
    Tru Tones vocalist
    Rookie Announcer (WIBS)

1968-Government Treasury Employee

1969-Radio Caribbean International
    (RCI)

1972-Radio Saint Lucia (RSL)

1976- CHMS Employment
    Halcyon Beach Club, Halcyon Days Hotel, Halcyon Sands, and
    Saint Lucian Hotel

1982-Cunard La Toc Hotel/Suites.

1984- Organizer - National Break-dance Competition (Mindoo Philip Park)

1985-Skyview Map Launch (large)
Helped with the setting up of RCI 101.1 FM with Mr. Tom Foster
Setting up Splash Nite Club

1987-Woy Calypso Album launch

1988-DSP Official Opening

1989- Launch of the following:
    Rameau Poleon Album
    Images Saint Lucia Video
    Skyview Map (Small version)

1991- Launch of the following:
    The King, the Dread & Buffalo album
    Fun in Paradise Video
    Opening of Sights & Sounds Music Shops

1993-Invader- "Kole Music Album".

1995- Launch of the Saint Lucia in your pocket - Tourism Guide

1997-DSP Home/Business Move

2002-Coffee Break at Sandals (Radio Saint Lucia)

2005-Sparrow Gold at Pigeon Island National Landmark

2008-The Agenda Talk Show (RSL)

2011- The Monarchs-Pt Seraphine

2013-Mr. Chairman (CTV)

2017-Ventured into writing.

2018-Launch of "My Story, Your Voice"

GLOSSARY

Acronyms:

CDC	-	Colonial Development Corporation
RC	-	Roman Catholic
CYO	-	Catholic Youth Organization
WIBS	-	Windward Islands Broadcasting Service.
RSL	-	Radio Saint Lucia
TTT	-	Top Twelve Tunes
45rpm	-	Revolutions per minute
RCI	-	Radio Caribbean International
Big A	-	Radio Antilles
HTS	-	Helen Television System
DBS	-	Daher Broadcasting Service
MBC	-	Mc Dowell Broadcasting Company
CHMS	-	Caribbean Hotel Management Services.
PR	-	Public Relations
STOP	-	St. Lucia Talent on Parade
HBC	-	Halcyon Beach Club
HDH	-	Halcyon Days Hotel
WIRL	-	West Indies Records Limited
QE11	-	Queen Elizabeth 11(Cruise liner)
DSP	-	David Samuels Promotions
PM	-	Prime Minister
M&C	-	Minvielle & Chastanet

WLBL	-	Windward & Leeward Brewery ltd.
EWTN	-	Eternal Word Television Network
OECS	-	Organisation of Eastern Caribbean States.
OAS	-	Organisation of American States
SLP	-	St. Lucia Labour Party
UWP	-	United Workers Party
MP	-	Member of Parliament
GOSL	-	Government of Saint Lucia
GG	-	Governor General
GH	-	Government House
VH	-	Victoria Hospital
GM	-	General Manager
GM	-	Golden Memories (RSL Program)
NIC	-	National Insurance Corporation
CSA	-	Civil Service Association
ECCO	-	Eastern Caribbean Copyright Association
NEMO	-	National Emergency Management Organization
UWI	-	University of the West Indies
SALCC	-	Sir Arthur Lewis Community College
NYC	-	National Youth Council
FRC	-	Folk Research Center
CDF	-	Cultural Development Foundation
VF	-	Vieux Fort (a town in the south)
KDA	-	Kenny Anthony
HMS	-	Hewanorra Music Society
BGR	-	British Government Representative
LBGT	-	Lesbian, Bi-sexual, Gay, Transgender
Messiah JC	-	A Fond Reference to Sir John

Kweyol Terms:

Kweyol	-	A form of broken french spoken
Jounen Kweyol	-	A day set aside to promote the dialect and culture
Radio Say Sa Nous	-	The "radio" is ours
Juk Bois	-	An expression used to probe someone
Woy	-	A Kweyol exclamation sound
Toujour Sou	-	Always drunk
Sab	-	A playing field just outside of Castries City
Belle Portwe	-	Beautiful photographs
Bon bon wasi	-	Stale cake -
Tet Chodé	-	Scotched head
Fanm Fol déyé yo	-	Mad woman behind them
Patois	-	Broken language
Faux-a-Chaux	-	Hot oven
Shac Shac	-	Percussion instruments
Senna	-	Herbal laxative
Gadé	-	witch doctor
Ti-Ponch	-	A rum mix
Encore	-	Repeat
La Rose	-	Flower festival after the celebration of St. Rose de Lima: A Catholic Saint
La Marguerite	-	The 2nd of two flower festivals, whose symbol is a purple rose
Chanteulle	-	Female singer
Lang mama nous	-	Our mother tongue
Malaway	-	the ordinary folk
Enwajay	-	Overly eager
Parlay	-	Speak

Pas worry ich moi	-	Don't worry my child
Yo pas Bondye	-	They are not God
Y paca kopan	-	He doesn't understand
Des Barras	-	A community in Babonneau
Oleon	-	A community in Dennery
Sey Tradition Nwel	-	Christmas tradition
Chartreuse	-	A pale green or yellow
Fuchsia	-	Purplish Red color
En Bas Gorge La	-	Reference to a violinist
Vye Nohm Sala	-	That Old Man
Kole	-	Come together
Jean Kaye	-	Home folks
Quick Quack	-	A Crusader Newspaper Column with some banter
Lank Mama Nous	-	Mother language
Cocky & Stocky	-	Political Characters
Bab Camawad	-	Friend's beard
Picong	-	Light hearted jokes, banter
Decalay	-	To destroy, defeat
Roro	-	Rumour, gossip

Printed in the United States
By Bookmasters